Functional Programming in PHP

Second Edition

by

Simon Holywell

 a php[**architect**] guide

Functional Programming in PHP—a php[architect] Guide

Second Edition: October 2016
ISBN - print: **978-1-940111-46-9**
ISBN - PDF: **978-1-940111-47-6**
ISBN - epub: **978-1-940111-48-3**
ISBN - mobi: **978-1-940111-49-0**
ISBN - safari: **978-1-940111-50-6**

Produced & Printed in the United States

Disclaimer

Written by
Simon Holywell

Published by
musketeers.me, LLC.
201 Adams Ave.
Alexandria, VA 22301 USA

240-348-5PHP (240-348-5747)
info@phparch.com
www.phparch.com

Editor-in-Chief
Oscar Merida

Technical Reviewers
Koen van Urk and Oscar Merida

Copy Editor
Kara Ferguson

Layout and Design
Kevin Bruce

Table of Contents

About the Author   VII

Acknowledgements   XI

Chapter 1.   Introduction   1
              Prerequisites   1
              Requirements   2
              For Users of Older PHP Versions   2
              Installing   3

Chapter 2.   What is Functional Programming?   7
              Let's See Some Code   9
              History   9
              Other Functional Implementations   15
              Commercial Uses   15
              What is Functional Programming Best for? 16
              The Benefits of Functional Programming   16
              Functional Basics   17

Chapter 3.	**Language Features**	**19**
	Types	20
	Functions	23
	Namespacing	39
	Recursion	40
	Map, Reduce, and Filter	42
	Memoization	47
	Generators	47
Chapter 4.	**Helpful Libraries**	**49**
	Library Installation	50
	The iter Library	52
Chapter 5.	**HHVM's Hack**	**55**
	Types	56
	Lambda Expressions	65
	Special (Magical) Attributes	66
	Conclusion	67
Chapter 6.	**Patterns**	**69**
	Head and Tail	70
	Flattening lists	70
	Handling Your NULLS	72
	Composition	75
	Partial Functions	76
	Pipelines	78
	Pattern Matching	80
	Functors	83
	Applicatives	88
	Monads	93

Chapter 7.   **Implementing the Theory**   **103**

   IP Address Restriction   103

   Functional Primitives   105

   A Domain Specific Language in PHP   108

Chapter 8.   **Event Driven Programming**   **117**

   ReactPHP Installation   118

   Getting Started   118

   Add Some Logging   119

   Introduce a Monad   119

   Callback Wrangling   122

   Wrap Up the Show   129

Chapter 9.   **Hazards of Functional Programming in PHP**   **131**

Chapter 10. **Advances in PHP**   **133**

   PHP 5.4   133

   PHP 5.5   134

   PHP 5.6   135

   PHP 7   137

   Further into the Future   140

Chapter 11. **Conclusion**   **143**

Appendix A. **Additional Notes**   **145**

   Understanding Type Signatures   145

   Using the UTF-8 Ellipsis   149

Appendix B. **Resources**   **151**

   PHP REPLs   151

Libraries   152
Other Functional Implementations   152
Online Courses (MOOC)   152

Glossary   **153**

Index   **159**

About the Author

Simon Holywell is a Senior Software Engineer at Aurion in Brisbane, Australia (*http://aurion.com*) and is passionate about web application development and motorcycles. His first public project was written with PHP 3, and since then, he has worked with every version of PHP and dabbled in Python, Scala, C, JavaScript, and more. He is also the author of SQLStyle.guide, and the ssdeep extensions for PHP's PECL, Facebook's HipHop Virtual Machine (HHVM), and MySQL.

Blog: *https://www.simonholywell.com*
Twitter: *@Treffynnon—http://twitter.com/Treffynnon*

For Marion, Damien, and Ariana.
Ngiyakuthanda! Ngiyabonga ntombenhle!

Acknowledgements

"Functional programming has become more and more popular in recent years because it promotes code that's safe, concise, and elegant."

—Martin Odersky
(Computer scientist and Scala programming language,
@odersky)

Many very supportive people were involved in the production of this book, and I would like to thank them for their keen insights and guidance. They helped me to take it from an idea to a fully-fledged book.

In particular, I would like to thank Beth Tucker Long who has been instrumental in bringing you this book right from the earliest of stages.

I also appreciate those who helped me formulate ideas and reviewed early drafts—especially Craig Bendell and Jamie Matthews.

To technical reviewers Oscar Merida and Koen van Urk, layout and diagram wrangler Kevin Bruce, Eli White, and Lori Ann Pannier for their contributions.

Cover Design

I worked through the concept for the front cover of the book and Kevin Bruce interpreted it into the clean design you see. Just what does it mean though?

For sometime now PHP has been associated with an elephant emblem. First designed by Vincent Pontier (a designer from France) it has been used by many to signify the PHP programming language. Some of the more well known uses are as plush toys and as the logo of the long standing PHP Classes site[1].

Whilst a friend walked Vincent through the possibilities of PHP in late 1998 he doodled with

[1] PHP Classes: *http://www.phpclasses.org*

the letters PHP on a piece of paper. Turning the paper sideways he noticed that the letters sort of formed a stylised outline of an elephant. Squint your eyes and you can probably see it too.

He would later create a clay model as a basis for the plush toys and gave them the name elephpant (note the extra P in the middle). For more information on the creation of the elephpants you should see the interview Khayrattee Wasseem conducted with Vincent on his site 7php.com[2].

To demonstrate this book's functional underpinnings the elephant is included inside parenthesis. The opening and closing parenthesis are shorthand for a function.

So in reality the cover image is a functional elephant.

If the existence of a plush toy piqued your interest then you can buy them directly from the original designer[3]. Many conferences, user groups and companies also create their own versions under licence.

It is worth pointing out that this is not an officially recognised emblem of PHP and indeed Postgresql use the pachyderm for their own logo albeit designed from a different angle. There have been numerous discussions about adopting the elephpant with Rasmus Lerdof having liked the idea in the past according to online gossip. It once even featured on the php.net logo download page.

[2] 7php.com: *http://7php.com/elephpant/*
[3] Adopt your elephpant: *http://elephant-php.com*

Chapter

1

Introduction

(*"I am in much dismay at having got into so amazing a quagmire
& botheration[...]"*

—Ada Lovelace (Mathematician, 1815–1852) discussing
mutability with Charles Babbage (created first concept of a
programmable computer, 1791–1871))

Over the course of the past twenty years or so, functional programming has seen a slow and steady growth. This has led to many languages adopting functional aspects, including the much-maligned PHP. As computer hardware and language support improves, it is important to begin learning the basics of functional programming. While it is true programming in this style requires a change in thinking, you will find some understanding of it has a positive impact on your object-oriented code as well.

Let us begin our journey through the functional aspects of the PHP language.

Prerequisites

You must have access to PHP version 5.4 or greater and command line access to the machine in question is incredibly beneficial. When writing, I used a Debian-based machine, and a similar POSIX computer is recommended, although not required.

One of the best things you can do while learning is to install a decent REPL on your machine as it will make it much easier to experiment with code as you follow along. REPL stands for read-eval-print loop, and it's basically a programming environment most commonly used on the command line. It allows you to try out algorithms easily without the need for an editor or even files to contain your code. Type code into it, hit return, and your code is executed with the result printed on screen.

There are a number of good REPLs out there, and I have had success with PsySH[1], Boris[2], and Facebook's PHPsh[3].

If you do not wish to install a REPL on your machine, you could use the online service 3V4L[4] but beware, of course, you will not have access to install extensions or libraries. This would only become a problem for you later on, however, as in the initial stages, we will be reviewing native language features.

As we progress through more functional programming in PHP, I will suggest useful PHP libraries and extensions. These are either installed via Composer [5] in the case of libraries or PECL[6] for extensions. If you are not already familiar with these, then it may pay to review them before continuing.

It goes without saying this book is not aimed at beginner PHP developers and some object-oriented experience is assumed. Having said that, of course, this is as gentle of an introduction as possible and represents a beginner guide to functional programming in PHP.

Requirements

PHP

- PHP 5.4+ (for some libraries, a later version might be required)

Other Software:

- Dependency management: Composer
- Extension/Library: functional-php
- Library: React/Partial
- Library: nicmart/Functionals

For Users of Older PHP Versions

It is certainly possible to write functional code and work through most of this book while using PHP 5.3.2 or greater—the first edition of this book was in fact written in PHP compatible with 5.3.2. There are a few things you may have to adapt in your code though, to ensure you don't access features that do not exist in the version of PHP you have installed.

Short array syntax will almost undoubtedly be the first syntax difference you will come across and fortunately it is very easy to adapt for usage on older versions of PHP. Short array syntax looks like the following sample:

```
$short_array = [1, 2, 3, 4, 5, 6, 7, 8, 9, 10];
```

Implemented in PHP versions less than 5.4 it would simply be converted to the following code:

```
$standard_array = array(1, 2, 3, 4, 5, 6, 7, 8, 9, 10);
```

[1]   PsySH: http://psysh.org
[2]   Boris: https://github.com/d11wtq/boris
[3]   PHPsh: http://phpsh.org
[4]   3V4L: http://www.3v4l.org
[5]   Composer Documentaion: http://getcomposer.org/doc/
[6]   PECL: http://pecl.php.net

Installing

Some of the chapters in this book will require you to install additional software before you can continue with the samples provided. This is reasonably easy although it does warrant some coverage here. Of these additional utilities some will be runtimes, others libraries and extensions.

Libraries are written using PHP userland code and tend to be slower to run, but easier for PHP developers to contribute to and maintain. They are generally packages of code that can be implemented using native PHP code calls and require statements. We will make use of Composer to greatly simplify the installation steps required to install these bundles of code.

The next step up in terms of performance and difficulty of installation is a PHP extension. Generally, these are sourced from the PECL repository of extensions although anyone can release an extension outside of the PECL structure themselves too. Extensions chosen from the PECL site are generally more likely to have had a code review from a PHP core developer prior to its approval for listing.

Finally we have other runtimes that are related to PHP; in this book we will stick to Facebook implemented HipHop Virtual Machine or HHVM for short. Not only does this runtime bring improved performance over native PHP through just in time compilation, but also extends PHP through the Hack language to provide an array of useful features.

As discussed, most of these additional pieces of software are relatively easy to install so for this set of instructions I am going to assume you are using, or have access to a Debian based Linux installation. A Vagrant box with a recent edition of Ubuntu on it would easily satisfy this requirement.

PHP Libraries

Installing libraries with PHP has never been easier with Composer replacing the now ageing PEAR repositories. This brings with it benefits like the ability to list a package and release it whenever you please. Conversely, there are disadvantages such as bad packages being listed beside good ones. Also PEAR had a code style guide packages needed to adhere to; any style is permissible with Composer. Having said that, many libraries have voluntarily adopted PSR-1[7] and PSR-2[8] standards.

You have the usual option of simply downloading a tarball of the package and extracting it to a directory, then manually pulling the files in with require statements. This, though, is discouraged in favor of the automation Composer provides.

Composer is a PHP phar archive you can easily install from the internet with two commands.

```
curl -sS https://getcomposer.org/installer | php
mv composer.phar /usr/local/bin/composer
```

You can now access Composer from anywhere on your machine via command line by simply entering `composer`.

To create a new Composer backed project you can call `composer init` and it will run through a wizard to configure your first `composer.json` file. Once this is complete it is possible to easily specify dependencies for your application by either editing the `composer.json` file directly or using the command line interface.

```
composer require vendor/package:0.3.*
```

This is where `vendor` is the vendor namespace such as `symfony`, `treffynnon`, or `j4mie` and `package` is the package namespace such as `silex`, `paris`, or `idiorm`. After the colon you can specify a version of the library you wish to use or your project implements.

[7]   PSR-1: Basic Coding Standard: http://www.php-fig.org/psr/psr-1/
[8]   PSR-2: Coding Style Guide: http://www.php-fig.org/psr/psr-2/

Alternatively if you do not know the name of the package you are interested in, you can search for it in an interactive fashion by calling `composer require` without any parameters.

Once your Composer file has all your requirements specified within it, you can commit it into source control and then anywhere you wish to run the project you can simply call `composer install` to have composer automatically install all your specified dependencies.

In addition to these dependency management features Composer also makes it easy to autoload the projects specified from within it. All you need to do is include one requirement statement to the top of your project's core/bootstrap file.

```
require 'vendor/autoload.php';
```

Now whenever your project is called it will automatically load the correct autoloaders to satisfy your application's dependency requirements. To speed up slow SPL autoloaders Composer also comes with an autoloader cache that it is recommended for use in production environments.

From the desired directory, when you want to create an autoload cache file you simply run the following command and Composer will automatically generate it for you.

```
composer dump-autoload -o
```

There is much more functionality available from Composer you can use to help you manage dependencies, but that small introduction should be enough to complete the tasks in this book and provide a jumping off point for your own research. Composer is the recommended way of specifying any dependencies for any application you may be working on as it makes installation and implementation fast and easy.

PECL Extensions

PHP extensions are usually formed of one or more C files that need to be compiled before the extension can be enabled and used. They may come from the PECL repository in which case the `pecl` command is very useful, or you can download them independently as tarballs.

The standard method to install a stable version of a PECL extension is to call:

```
pecl install package_name
```

Should the package be in alpha or beta state, you can easily install it by appending the release status to the install command like so:

```
pecl install package_name-beta
```

or

```
pecl install package_name-alpha
```

Another option is to set your `pecl` command line manager to always install beta or alpha packages if they are available:

```
pecl config-set preferred_state beta
```

or

```
pecl config-set preferred_state alpha
```

You can also easily install a specific version of a PECL extension by including the number after the package name:

```
pecl install package_name-0.0.2
```

Besides alpha and beta versions of the extensions there can also be devel and stable releases.

PECL can also install extensions from the archive packages, which can be downloaded from the PECL website:

```
pecl install package_name-1.0.0.tgz
```

To manually build and install a PECL extension is also relatively easy from an extracted tarball directory:

```
cd package_name
phpize
./configure
make
make install
```

So once the extension is built using any of the aforementioned methods you will also need to enable it in the php.ini file by adding:

```
extension=package_name.so
```

It should be noted here, if you are using this extension with a website rather than on the PHP CLI then you will need to restart your web server for the new PHP configuration to take effect.

PHP extensions provide a way of creating fast running functionality for PHP via a C interface to the core of the language itself. C code runs much faster than its PHP counterpart, so this is one means of speeding up some applications.

HHVM

There are two ways to install HipHop Virtual Machine (HHVM) on a Linux machine with manual compilation (time consuming) and installing a ready made binary. As we are not going to be making use of any HHVM extensions we can happily use a pre-built package. To make things even easier, the code we will implement on HHVM is available in the version provided by Facebook for Ubuntu 14.04.

This makes installing the HHVM alternative runtime as simple as a few calls to Ubuntu's apt-get package management system.

```
# installs add-apt-repository
sudo apt-get install software-properties-common

sudo apt-key adv --recv-keys \
 --keyserver hkp://keyserver.ubuntu.com:80 0x5a16e7281be7a449
sudo add-apt-repository 'deb http://dl.hhvm.com/ubuntu trusty main'
sudo apt-get update
sudo apt-get install hhvm
```

You should now be able to call hhvm directly on the command line like you would with PHP's CLI. A word of caution though; the just-in-time compiler or JIT that HHVM employs to speed up the running of PHP and Hack code is not active on the command line by default. This makes sense because there is a startup cost of bytecode compilation with the JIT turned on that would only make sense to incur on long running scripts.

That said, if you do want to force the HHVM JIT on for the command line, you do so by passing a parameter to the HHVM command line client.

```
hhvm -vEval.Jit=1
```

HHVM is a more simplified means of speeding up code than a PHP extension and it also brings with it a horde of goodies in the Hack language additions to PHP. The primary interest in HHVM for this book are the data structures and little pieces of syntactic sugar Hack adds to the base PHP language.

Hack can also be installed on other Linuxes and MacOS, but Ubuntu was the preferred platform during development of HHVM. Users of both Haiku OS[9] and Windows need not apply!

---

[9] *Haiku OS is an open source reincarnation of the now long forgotten, but once much loved BeOS prized for its concurrency (something of interest to functional programmers) leading to an ultra-responsive user interface*

Chapter

2

What is Functional Programming?

> *"Programming where your entire program is a single referentially transparent expression composed of other referentially transparent expressions. No side effects. No mutability. No global mutable state."*
>
> —Rúnar Bjarnason (Functional programmer, *@runarorama*)

It is difficult to categorically define functional programming as all functional languages vary, and there is not a universally agreed upon specification. Couple that with the fact there are varying opinions amongst programmers as to what makes a functional language, and you have a conundrum. To confuse matters further, many languages have functional elements or primitives defined in them.

While perilous, I will make an attempt at a very simplified explanation of a core tenet. Programming in a functional way is essentially coding without any assignment of values. There, I said it! Of course, there's a lot more to it, but this is the most simplistic—and also the most mind blowing—statement for those of us from an imperative programming background like PHP.

This is a very simplified allusion to the functional approach of removing state from your programs and emphasizing purity. It is, of course, also an incendiary challenge to your current programming practices. As your understanding of functional programming grows you will begin to understand more encompassing descriptions of what constitutes a functional piece of code.

To begin with, it is important to define what imperative programming means so there is a good base to build upon. Imperative programming is often thought of as the diametric opposite of functional programming allowing us to eliminate it from the description of what functional programming actually is. It is a style where the programmer tells the computer step by step exactly what it should do to complete a computation or program.

You may think this just applies to procedural PHP (code that does not make use of PHP's object oriented constructs and functions), but you would be wrong. Simon Peyton Jones of Haskell fame describes imperative programming as[1]:

> *"…a sequence of steps. Every line says do this, then do this, do this. When you call a method often there are no results [returned]…because the sole reason for calling it is to have an effect on the world. To change the state of something."*

He points out a very noteworthy property of imperative programming—there are hidden changes to state. This means if you call a method in an imperative program you cannot be sure if it will just compute the result given your arguments or whether it will also adjust the state of the program. As a functional program seeks to be pure, these changes in state must be eliminated.

A number of people describe functional programming based on this property of no changes to state. One such person is Erik Meijer who has a love of Haskell and has worked on the C# programming language, among others. He describes functional programming as being[2]:

> *"…about programming using mathematical functions. Whenever you supply it with the same argument it returns the same result. Every time I execute it, it will give me the same result."*

This description of functional programming will make more sense once you have had more exposure to functions as it alludes to referential transparency which is addressed deeper in the book, after discussing the base concepts.

So just how do you get anything done in a functional style? Surely, without assignment statements nothing is possible? How do you pass values around in your programs?

The answer is incredibly simple; values can be passed from function to function as arguments and return values. Extending this idea further, we can have functions that return functions or accept functions as parameters. The more you think about it, the more powerful it becomes.

These combinations of functions express the program's intent succinctly and cleanly. The immutable constructs help to ensure side effects cannot work their way into a functional program. Here I am referring to the avoidance of variable assignments, which is the fundamental basis of imperative languages.

Humble functions are far more useful and powerful than most object-oriented PHP programmers give them credit for.

[1] Simon Peyton Jones—Haskell is useless: *http://youtu.be/iSmkqocn0oQ?t=1m23s*
[2] Erik Meijer: Functional Programming : *http://youtu.be/z0N1aZ6SnBk?t=16m44s*

Let's See Some Code

Wipe that look of incredulity from your face; here is a simple imperative example which sums all the integers from one to ten:

```
$sum = 0;
for($i = 1; $i <= 10; $i++) {
    $sum += $i;
}
// $sum = 55
```

Versus a more functional style using PHP's `range()` and `array_sum()` function to generate an array from 1 to 10 and sum all of its values:

```
array_sum(range(1, 10)); // 55
```

Here we have hit upon a key concept and benefit of functional programming. Instead of detailing the steps required to sum the numbers, we have merely described the result we want when given a set of values.

We have also managed to avoid the use of state-tracking variables (`$sum` in the imperative example) and automatically divided the units of work up into reusable functions. If we need a `range()` elsewhere, we can easily reuse the same code.

Conversely in the imperative example, we are required to do all the leg work such as looping and maintaining state using variable assignments. Perhaps this could be considered somewhat like writing a recipe, where the constants are your ingredients list and the loop is equivalent to the step-by-step directions.

Continuing the food-based analogy, we might suggest the functional example is more akin to ordering a meal at a restaurant where you simply pick from a menu. Although, like a good pizzeria, you can always add more toppings yourself!

As you can probably see, functional programming and well-designed, object-oriented code can be very similar in that they both aspire to encapsulate and break down units of work into smaller reusable chunks.

History

The history of functional programming and indeed computing, in general, is entirely dependent on the work completed in the fields of mathematics and logic. It is possible to trace back the collective accumulation of knowledge in these areas to some of the earliest recorded philosophers and mathematicians.

To mention both Socrates and Aristotle is not out of place when considering their contributions to the understanding of logic. That is to say, the roots of computing extend way back beyond 400BC. Some time later in mid-200BC Archimedes would write some of the very earliest beginnings of calculus, which were later discovered in a codex known as the Archimedes Palimpsest. It had been overwritten with religious text in the 13th century and therefore lost to humanity. Luckily most of it has been recovered through the use of various imaging equipment including X-Rays, but much too late to inform the calculus visionaries we will meet next.

From a functional point of view however, it begins to get interesting in 1666 and 1675 when both Isaac Newton and Gottfried Leibniz (respectively) documented the earliest formalisms of calculus. This mathematical discovery was the foundation of all functional thinking and an important part of computational history in general.

Supposedly, unbeknownst to either man, they had both been working on their papers at the same time. Purely by coincidence, they arrived at similar conclusions at a similar time. In reality, it is more likely the theoretical groundwork had already been laid by prior minds and the conditions were right for someone to make the next logical step forward.

Never the less some controversy surrounds this part of history as Newton had been working on calculus, but did not publish anything until 1693. Leibniz, on the other hand, published in 1684 and was most likely aware of Newton's earlier work as they were both members of the Royal Society in London.

When asked to formally determine who had invented calculus the Society stated that while Leibniz had been first to publish, Newton had created it. Disturbingly, Newton was president of the Royal Society in London at the time, and therefore would have had influence over its final decision. Later, the Society would make claims of plagiarism against Leibniz, further tarnishing his name and would eventually cement his relegation to the annals of history.

Despite this, his impact upon mathematics and calculus is clear. Leibniz's notation for calculus is still in use today and he would later go on to produce a calculation machine. This machine was based upon the binary ideas from ancient China. This would prove to be the basis of modern computing as we know it.

Gottlob Frege would go on to further develop calculus by defining the first predicate calculus. Some of the developments he worked on are still in use to this day. His main concern though was to prove mathematics could be completely described by logic. Unfortunately for him, this turned out to be false.

Frege's Basic Law V described a set logic which made defining membership easy. Unfortunately for Frege, it also allowed Bertrand Russell to find an inconsistency. Famously known as Russell's Paradox, it relayed a self-referential set: "the set of things x that such that x is not a member of x." This tongue twister would produce a set that was simultaneously not a member and a member of itself. This discovery stumped Frege and left him floundering with weak arguments and workarounds for the issue.

Despite this, logicians continued to work towards a system that would describe the entire world. In the world of philosophy this leads to the formation of the hugely influential Vienna circle. The assembled members would discuss the division of statements into near enough two categories. On one side they would include statements which could not be observed, and on the other those that could be. Anything metaphysical is meaningless and rejected as a logical mistake or reduced to empirical statements that could be

The Story of George Boole

George Boole was an English mathematician and logician who gave his name to Boolean logic. Born into a working class family he was not the typical child prodigy of his era. He taught himself mathematics and logic by spending extended periods in a reference library. Later on, he would become the first professor of mathematics at Queens College, Cork in Ireland. This is where he would meet his wife Mary Everest (a niece of George Everest whom Mt. Everest is named after). Interestingly while the mountain is pronounced Ever-est, their family name was actually pronounced as Eve-rest.

It was at this same institution Boole caught a cold that would lead to his eventual death. While walking to give a lecture, he was saturated by a heavy rain storm. After giving the lecture in wet clothes he became ill and was cared for by his wife. Unfortunately, she subscribed to a theory, common at the time, that cause is cure. To this end, she threw buckets of cold water over him as he lay stricken in bed. The theory held that if it was cold water that caused the illness, then more of the same would cure it. His condition worsened and on the 8th of December 1864 he died. A highly illogical end to befall a seminal logician!

While not a direct contributor to the history of functional programming he did influence the progress of logic and worked extensively on Boolean algebra. He did teach himself calculus, but it was not his primary area of study.

The Boolean algebra he devised was used to layout logical arguments and ascertain an answer or outcome. The idea was to create a language applicable to any logical statement, to determine the validity of that statement. This supported further discoveries in logic and mathematics.

proven by scientific investigation. An example of a metaphysical statement would be "all art is pointless"–it can neither be proven true nor false.

In the interim, no major breakthroughs were found in the field of calculus. Logicians were hard at work though, formulating systems and proofs to describe the world.

During this period they employed a student to oversee the discussions by halting conversations leading to metaphysical discourse. Initially they would yell "Metaphysik", but as Rudolph Carnap would later relay they swiftly shortened it to just "M". As discussion progressed further, "he was shouting 'M' so much we got sick of it so it was changed to 'no-M' whenever we said something legitimate." In other words, most discussions lead to a metaphysical discussion. This brought Carnap to the realization there could be many logics, and not just one universal logic.

Around the same time, an eminent German mathematician named David Hilbert was setting out with a similar goal in the world of mathematics. In the late 1920's he was passionate about solving the Entscheidungs Problem by proving everything can be described by mathematical logic. Hilbert was certain everything could be reduced to either true or false.

Somewhat famously, in 1930 a student of the Vienna Circle, Kurt Gödel, delivered his completeness theorem which helped to bolster Hilbert's hypothesis. This, however, was short lived when the very next day Gödel also discussed his first incompleteness theorem, which undermined the very foundations of Hilbert's assertions. It is now universally recognized the Hilbert cohorts were incorrect and there are some problems logic cannot solve or describe.

So, how did Gödel upset the apple cart? *This statement is not provable.* Simple!

If the statement can be proven then it is false, but it states it cannot be proven so it must be true. This statement cannot be decided because it is both true and false at the same time. You've probably heard of a similar statement before called The Liar Paradox. This predates Gödel by at least 2,000 years with some sources suggesting roots in 600BC to 400BC. "A man says that he is lying. Is what he says true or false?" Over time this has been distilled down to "this sentence is false" and is remarkably similar to the basis of Gödel's incompleteness theorem. This though, is a layman's simplification as Gödel proved this was a paradox in all logic.

He proved this to be the case across two theorems using a logic expression system he designed himself. This may seem like the easiest paradox to modern eyes, but at the time Gödel was at the cutting edge of logic. To further prove the undecideability of the Entschiedungs Problem it was necessary to define effective computing. This lead to a number of systems being devised at once.

In 1932, the first system was proposed by Alonzo Church in the form of the lambda calculus. He saw the potential in his new definition and wrote:

"There may, indeed be other applications of the system than its use as a logic."

Given that lambda calculus would go on to be the foundation for functional programming it is certainly fair to say he was right. Using lambda calculus as a base Church was able to put forward a problem without an effectively calculable answer. Again, the simplicity is striking; given a lambda expression, determine if it will loop forever. It can't be done!

Gödel was working on his own system of logic around the same time of recursive functions. While it may not look the same as Gödel's formalisms, recursion is a core component of functional programming.

Also at this time Alan Turing was introduced to Gödel's undecideability problem and—just as Gödel— he came to the conclusion: to work on the Entschiedungs Problem you must define a system of effective calculability. He devised the Turing Machine which could calculate all the numbers naturally considered computable. By this I mean numbers a human could calculate with a pencil and paper.

This allowed Turing along with Alonzo Church to show both lambda expressions and Turing Machines are functionally equivalent. Working with Church, Turing would go on to create the first program to compute lambda expressions. They wrote a paper together in 1937 known as the Church-Turing Thesis which showed both techniques were equivalent and equally justified. Turing even went so far as to say "Church's calculus…allows [Turing] 'Machines' which generate computable functions to be replaced by the more convenient λ-definitions." Based on this we could be daring and say Turing preferred functional programming! A presumptuous extrapolation you might say, but certainly he developed a fondness for those formalisms.

In the 1940's Alonzo Church was working on a paper describing typed lambda calculus and its formal proofs. Independently Turing was also working a similar proof which went unpublished, although it serves as a good indication he saw mileage in the techniques.

It's interesting to note the world received no less than four techniques to describe effective computation: Alonzo Church's lambda calculus, Alan Turing's Turing machine, Kurt Gödel's recursive functions, and the hitherto undiscussed combinatory logic from Haskell Curry. This is no coincidence and merely a consequence of the conditions being right for such a set of formalisms to be produced.

The preparatory groundwork had been completed and the world of logic was ready for fresh ideas and discoveries. This explains the discoveries being so close to each other in time, even if they did not know others were also working on the same ideas.

Back to Haskell's combinatory logic for a moment and its function composing formalisms. Primitive functions are combined to create more powerful constructs; a principle you will see throughout functional programming. Published in 1927, it predates the other forms from Turing et. al. by a number of years.

There is some debate that the first to create a proof of combinatory logic may have been a Russian by the name of Moses Schönfinkel. This has an effect on the name given to the functional programming technique of currying, too, with some suggesting it should be Schönfinkelization to recognize his earlier discovery. Unfortunately, the story of Schönfinkel is a sad one. Aside from this paper, relatively little is known of his work. He was a member of Hilbert's group and it was with their assistance he managed to have this paper published in 1924. A few years later he moved back to Russia from Göttingen and reports filtered back in 1927 he was mentally ill and confined to a sanitarium. It is not known precisely when, but sometime during 1942 he died a pauper.

All his papers were burnt by his neighbors for heat, so it will never be known what he had been working on.

It was also around this time during World War Two Alan Turing was famously based at Bletchley Park where he worked to crack the Enigma code among a team of Britain's greatest minds. The first break in the Enigma code was established with the so called Green Key in 1940, and later the Red key of the Luftwaffe was also established. A recent feature film, The Imitation Game, starring Benedict Cumberbatch as Turing details this period.

It did not take the Nazis long to begin using a more sophisticated encryption in the form of new device called the Geheimschreiber (secret writer). Turing worked to break Tunny (the British code name for the secret writer) and devised a technique called Turingery in 1942. Implementing Turingery on a larger scale informed the design of the first programmable electronic computer by the team of Tommy Flowers and Max Newman.

Known as the Colossus computer it was quite different to the device you are likely reading this book on right now. It used thermionic valves (mostly unused these days except in overpriced hifi equipment and professional guitar amplifiers) to perform Boolean operations as transistors might be used today. These controlled a series of relays and stepping motors making it a very active and physical machine—you certainly would have been able to hear it working!

Modern machines are entirely different, with discreet and solid state electronics powering our computing today. In many machines today the only moving parts are cooling fans and perhaps the odd peripheral you've plugged in via USB. The replacement of hard drives with solid state drives and the disc drive ceding transportable data to memory sticks or cloud storage has left machines virtually silent.

A functioning replica of the Colossus can be seen at The National Museum of Computing at Bletchley Park in England. The original and its blueprints were destroyed and the information remained classified until the 1970's.

So although Turing's work undoubtedly helped it is a stretch to say he worked on the project directly. He was instead working on a secure telephone system which would encipher speech. Codenamed Delilah, it unfortunately lacked long distance capability and was not completed in time to be used during WWII. This lead Turing back to working in computing and he produced the first in depth paper on a stored-program computer, narrowly beating John Von Neumann's draft which had been circulating towards publication. Many of the ideas contained in Von Neumann's draft are said to be those of Turing in retrospect anyway.

In addition, Turing was famously working on artificial intelligence problems. To him it was not a case of if a machine could be intelligent, but when. In order to determine when this milestone was reached Turing devised a simple test (well simple for a human, but not necessarily a machine) now known as The Turing Test. If a machine can communicate with a human audience in a manner indistinguishable from a person, then it could be considered intelligent. Although it sounds simple to us, it is worth noting speech and elaborate communication are unique to human beings on earth. Even primates that have been taught sign language have never asked their handlers a solitary question, perhaps due to limits in their cognition or simply due to the fact language is extremely hard to master.

There have been recent claims the Turing test has been met by a computer program. Much like a car manufacturers fuel economy claims, actual real world usage does not yield the same results as those noted in the laboratory. The test was completed under a set of conditions which sought to game the test.

Unfortunately, Turing's great mind and contributions to the war effort would not protect him from persecution. In 1950's England it was illegal to engage in homosexual acts and after mentioning to the police that a burglary at his home might have been committed by an associate of his boyfriend, he was swiftly arrested. He was found guilty when the case came to court and sentenced to prison or a commuted sentence on condition of having chemical castration. Turing opted for the medical intervention while his boyfriend received a seven month suspended sentence, perhaps due his being younger than Turing.

Although his family disputes it, in 1954 Turing is believed to have committed suicide by poisoning his daily apple with cyanide. Some have pointed out a gold electro-plating experiment he had setup could have produced a lethal amount of cyanide. An alternative explanation could be he set it up so as to protect his mother and give her plausible deniability of her son's suicide. Turing's legacy is well-known in the computing world and has recently been promoted to a larger audience with the release of the feature film, *The Imitation Game*. Before this there was a wide scale campaign in 2009 to obtain an official apology from the British government for the way Turing was treated. In 2013 he was granted a posthumous pardon.

The next major advance of functional computing came in 1958 with John McCarthy's LISP programming language based upon Alonzo Church's lambda calculus. The language's name is a play on the term list processing, which makes sense given the language's reliance on lists.

Interestingly, LISP would go onto be the de facto standard in the artificial intelligence community. McCarthy used Alonzo Church's ideas to work upon artificial intelligence ideas Turing must have pondered prior to his death.

Many languages and computer science, in general, have a lot to thank LISP for. It brought new ideas to light in the form of dynamic typing, data tree structures, conditionals, recursion and higher order functions. Other languages may have included approximately similar functions, but never in such a cohesive fashion.

LISP is instantly recognizable from its S-expressions which look like lists. They are written as a list with the function name first and the arguments following separated by spaces. Over the years there have been many LISP variants released with Common Lisp, Scheme, and Clojure being the most well-known today.

If you're interested in playing with writing your own programming language then one place to start is with a LISP of your own. A number of resources are available on the web to create LISP interpreters with C, Python and C++. In the PHP world limited work has been completed with projects like Mathias Verraes' Lambdalicious, Igor Wiedler's Lisphp, and Tamreen Kahn's Pharen cross compiler written in PHP.

As time progressed there was little movement in the functional space. The existing languages were still mostly confined to the academic arena with a relatively small user base. As mentioned previously, the artificial intelligence community did work in a functional style with LISP.

Outside of this you need to skip forward in time until the telecommunications industry began looking for a fault tolerant system. After all, they couldn't have customer's calls, pages, and messages dropping out or going undelivered. The Ericsson telephone company spearheaded early developments in the functional space for the telecommunications sector. In their labs they worked on a language which would ease the problems their industry faced, with uptime and reliability being the most important.

Out of these investigations in the mid-eighties the Erlang programming language was born. Based on Prolog and to begin with implemented in the language it would go on to power all of Ericsson's infrastructure. Later, though, as Erlang was a proprietary language Ericsson decided to cease using their own language in the late 1990's! Following the departure of key members of their language team in 1998 (no doubt in protest) Ericsson open sourced the Erlang language and made it possible for it to be used internally again.

> It is also worth noting Erlang is not short for Ericsson Language, but rather it is named after a computer scientist named Erlang. Although, it does serve the dual purpose quite admirably.

Since its creation Erlang has been used by numerous household names in a number of industry sectors. One of the most well-known recent uses of Erlang is as the base language for the CouchDB NoSQL server. This storage system uses map and reduce statements to make it possible to extricate the correct information—the significance of this will become clearer later. Well, at least in relation to functional programming anyway!

At around the same time as Erlang was being designed with a practical purpose in mind, another functional language was in it's infancy. Designed by committee and open source at its outset, Haskell has gone on to become arguably the most well-known pure functional language. In the beginning however it was not even able to output anything—it was a pure and solid state box.

This reflects its beginnings as an experiment and an educational tool. As IO (input/output) is inherently stateful they grappled with the problem of defending their code from outside influences. You want to be able to access information such as a database or a text file on disk in such a way that it does not introduce stateful operations.

If you have a knowledge of electronics then this could be considered similar to amplification circuits, in a simplified way. You need a power source to boost the signal, but it is important no noise be introduced from the power source to the signal. There really is only a passing resemblance so don't delve too deeply in!

Haskell now powers projects in the open source world and even in banking. A couple of projects you might have heard of include Pandoc and xmonad. It is still relatively small with many companies preferring to stick with familiar tools and methodologies.

This set the scene for the creation of the Scala programming language in 2004 on both the Java and .NET runtimes. It allowed a functional language to be used in existing infrastructures. The .NET version ceased in 2012 with language development becoming focused on the JVM (Java Virtual Machine). While these underpinnings sped up the development and adoption of the language, they did come with a cost. Neither platform was designed to host a functional language. This has led to some difficulties and shortcomings, but nothing warranting further discussion in the context of this book.

Unlike Haskell, the Scala language is not purely functional and it is possible to write very elegant object oriented code in it. This is another one of its attractions; a familiar methodology neatly executed. As it also runs on the JVM, it is possible to use Java packages from Scala code directly.

It could be argued Scala is more trendy than Haskell with companies such as Twitter, LinkedIn, Foursquare, and The Guardian making use of Scala in their core product offerings. Again this is very subjective! Twitter has written a number of onboarding guides for new engineers which serve as handy learning resources [3].

As these languages have evolved, the level of interest has increased. This can, at least partially, be attributed to the increased need for parallel processes to harness multi core and node architectures. Functional code eases the shared mutable state problem imperative code can suffer from. This has made it increasingly attractive as architectures become more and more complicated to handle greater load.

More recent converts to functional code could easily have learned online from a MOOC with a number of courses touching on Haskell and Scala. These can serve as good introductions to those languages and Scala in particular has a number of good books written for learners of the language.

The history of functional programming is irrevocably intertwined with discoveries in mathematics and logic. Off the back of those advancements programming and computing itself were created. While functional style programs are still not as popular as their state filled counterparts, adoption appears to be steadily increasing.

Other Functional Implementations

The spectrum of languages that might consider themselves as implementing functional constructs is quite broad. In terms of pure functional languages, Haskell is possibly the most well-known. Somewhere in the middle are languages like Scala and Clojure which contain both imperative as well as functional styles.

Then much further out on the fringes, there are languages like our beloved and oft-vilified PHP, which has slowly been acquiring the basic ingredients for functional programming.

For the sake of contrast, here is the same `sum` example in Haskell, which is as simple as:

```
sum[1..10]
```

As you can see, the syntax makes it very easy to clearly express the program in a minimal number of characters.

Commercial Uses

One often cited benefit for a functional approach is in the construction of domain specific languages (DSLs). The functional constructs in most languages successfully reduce the amount of low-level work required when parsing a language as built-in type handling and pattern matching enable fast and complex parsers to be written in fewer lines of code.

[3]   Scala School: https://twitter.github.io/scala_school/

The advantage of this is it greatly eases maintenance chores and makes the code simpler to understand.

A well-known commercial example of this can be found in the Functional Payout Framework for exotic trades at Barclays Bank. Written in Haskell, it defines a DSL for mathematicians to create trading applications upon. The compact and flexible functional implementations allow the team to react more effectively and quickly to user requests for new features. There were some concerns for the team at the outset of the project, chief among which was the need to interface with other legacy systems written in languages such as C. Not only was this easily completed with Haskell, but it worked out to be a bonus as it prevented tight coupling of the components.

Probably the most well-known commercial use of functional programming is the inception of the Erlang language at Ericsson, which was specifically designed to improve productivity through a high-level symbolic language. Due to the stringent reliability and concurrency demands of telecommunications, Ericsson ruled out the array of functional languages at the time with LISP and Prolog being the front runners.

Erlang has since been adopted by many commercial users and powers numerous mission critical pieces of hardware. It's probably the biggest success story in terms of commercial adoption and continued use in its target domain.

A more recent example comes from Twitter, which is using Scala to handle a number of key features for their social service. While Scala is not a purely functional language (it has object-oriented support as well), it is certainly well equipped to do so. Some of the features you use every day on Twitter are powered by Scala, including the store of user relationships, searching for users by name or interests, and the "who to follow" fuzzy suggestions Twitter provides. The abstractions allowed by functional programming in Scala have also meant it is being used in many other areas as well, such as the streaming API, the Kestrel queuing mechanism, and their geo systems.

What is Functional Programming Best for?

As you will see, anything which can be done imperatively can also be completed using functional methodologies. Although each methodology has its advantages you can view them as simply another way of slicing the cake.

There is no golden rule recommending functional-style programming in certain situations or object-oriented programming in others. Functional programming is not a framework or design pattern, but a Turing complete programming methodology. To this end, as you familiarize yourself with functional programming, you will develop an innate sense of when a particular methodology is best employed to solve a problem. It is worth noting this will be different for each programming language and working in functional programming versus object-oriented programming in Scala is very different compared to the same in PHP.

In the PHP world, due to the bias towards object-oriented programming, functional programming is mostly used for list (array) processing, but it does not stop us from exploring more complex functional constructs as you will see further on.

The Benefits of Functional Programming

So how does removing features from your imperative language help you?

With the ever increasing popularity of functional programming, it is important to keep pace. Insights gleaned from your exploration of functional code can be applied in object-oriented programming as well.

One regularly quoted rule states the increase in the legibility of a program improves as the level of abstraction rises by virtue of the succinct code it encourages. It is also often said a side effect of these attributes is an increase in productivity with less typing and no global state to construct in your mind, helping to free your time for the more difficult problems.

Testing your code becomes much easier because all values are final, which means you do not have to contend with side effects. There is no particular order to maintain or global state which needs to be put into place. All you need to do is pass in the correct arguments, and you will always get the same result.

This concept is often described as referential transparency, which basically means you can replace any function call with the value it returns, and the resulting algorithm will remain the same. Therefore, instead of range(), we could use a static array and still get the same result:

```
array_sum([ 1, 2, 3, 4, 5, 6, 7, 8, 9, 10 ]); // 55
```

Substituting static values into the imperative example would be impossible (don't contort yourselves proving me wrong!), and this is where programming in a functional-style really shines. Each function, given the same input, will always return the same value.

It should not be underestimated how much easier these functions are to test than their state-filled counterparts. There is less time wasted mocking global state and when a test fails, it will always fail. This makes it far easier to debug any test. Reproducing the bug does not require long chains of actions to surface due to the functional program's avoidance of any global state and adoption of encapsulation for its components. If a function is not returning the correct values, then it is always incorrect.

While it is not usually an issue with PHP, functional programs help to prevent race conditions between threads or processes. Maintaining a functional style allows you to program these types of applications with confidence (well, almost!). The importance of parallel processing continues to grow with the advancement of computer hardware.

Computers are gaining more and more power by increasing the number of cores the central processing units contain. If your software is to take advantage of this power, then you will need to account for simultaneous processing.

This is where functional programming's abandonment of assignment statements really helps to protect you from process locking or attempting to update the same locations in memory. It also serves to make the order of execution irrelevant, as without state to update, a function will always return the same value. It is when you allow state to creep into code that breaking jobs off into parallel processes falters.

Additional benefits of functional programming which do not generally apply to PHP—so we won't discuss them here—are hot code deployment and machine optimization of code.

Functional Basics

Despite PHP being inherently imperative, it can support a basic functional style of programming. To make it easier to learn, it is best to eschew some aspects of the language to emulate a purer functional one.

- Avoid changing state—even within a function.
- Attempt to keep functions to one line or as short as possible.
- Break problems down to their smallest units and turn these into reusable functions.
- Remove control statements from your code.
- As it is worth repeating; avoid state and do not use variable assignments!

You want to essentially create a little black box function which will always return the same value when given the correct arguments.

PHP has a number of language features to help form the basis of programming in this style. Probably the most useful is the lambda function, which makes it easier to deal with code passing functions around as variables. Additionally, language functions such as `array_map()` and `array_reduce()` are very useful for applying functions to lists of values.

There are no immutable value types or statically-typed variables in PHP so it is up to your implementation to protect your functional code from changing state.

As you begin to work in a functional way, you will need access to more primitives for the more complex operations you will encounter. Luckily, the path has been previously trodden, and there are a number of libraries we will cover later.

Chapter

3

Language Features

"Recursion is the GOTO of functional programming."

—Erik Meijer (Computer Scientist, *@headinthebox*)

Despite PHP's reputation for being a little lack luster in stringent programming environments, it is reasonably well featured. Most of its power came in versions 5.3 and above, but since PHP 5 it has been headed in a good direction. Notice I said "good" and not "the right" direction! As version 5 has progressed there has been a number of new features added to the language that have also greatly eased development with PHP.

While it is true a lot of these features could have been implemented in more optimal ways to support functional style programming, they none the less exist. Outside of their varied shortcomings they actually provide a viable basis for functional programming in PHP itself.

This is one of the more important things to realize early on; although the base capability is there, you do not get any high level niceties. If you want more power and convenience, you will have to write the code to facilitate this yourself (or co-opt a library). Sometimes this might be as simple as wrapping a function call and other times you might find yourself writing a library or two.

This is both the fun and currently the difficulty with PHP. If you have an idea where to start, then being productive in functional style PHP is relatively easy. If not, then you could easily find yourself bogged down in high level library creation.

That is the purpose of this book; to give you shortcuts to the best bits of the language and the third-party libraries to make functional programming in PHP more enjoyable and even fun! To begin with we will simply go through the relevant base of features of PHP itself.

These range from the basics of types and function definitions through to more involved operations, such as map and reduce. Along the way we will touch upon recursion, closures, and lambda functions.

PHP can be used for purely functional programming and this can lead to increased productivity and reduced errors. The properties of good functional code also make it easily testable. Once you have stepped through the features in this chapter you will see the base potential the language has for this style.

I liken it to an adventure, such as those undertaken by Sjaak Lucassen who pretty much rode the entire world on a Yamaha R1. A super-bike taken down barely recognizable quagmires of roads—as far from its race track habitat as an R1 has probably ever been. Plenty of people will tell you it is impractical or down-right impossible. I am here to tell you it is very possible, and in many ways can be a very elegant method of solving the problem—even in PHP!

Types

The typing in PHP will serve as a starting point for the concepts in this chapter.

Types, typing, and type systems all refer to the concept of values having a type and not just contents. This means if you assign a word as the contents of a value it will be given the type of string. If you assigned it a whole number then it would normally be given a type of integer.

Programming languages like PHP utilize a type system just like this, where the type is inferred from the value assigned to the variable. If you assign the word `"test"` to a variable, PHP will automatically infer the type should be a string. This, however, is just half of the story of dynamic typing. Other languages use a system where you specify the type of a variable at the point of its definition. Yet other languages use a combination of them both.

In PHP there are the following scalar data types available to the parser. Scalar types are the most basic type and include simple things such as numbers and text.

- Boolean—`true` or `false`
- integer—Whole numbers (including negative numbers)
- float—Floating point numbers (decimals)
- double—Alias of `float`
- string—Textual information

As the needs of a program become more complex, values must be increased in power to accommodate their compound nature.

- array—Ordered map or key/value list
- object—Instance of a class

Finally, PHP also has some special types it defines for specific language features.

- resource—A reference to an external resource such as a file handle
- NULL—Represents a variable with no value
- callable—As of PHP 5.4 a variable to can be treated as a function

None of these types can be explicitly set as a type directly on a PHP variable. As mentioned earlier if you set a variable to be a whole number PHP will automatically make the variable a type of integer.

PHP does offer casts, which can make it possible to cause the type of the value to change. For example, if you cast a string of "10" to an integer the PHP parser will convert the type of the value to an integer (10) like so:

```
$a = '10';
var_dump($a); // string(10)
var_dump((int) $a); // int(10)
```

This can be especially useful when trying to trigger a class's __toString() method.

```
class MyString {
    public function __toString() {
        return 'Indoda';
    }
}
$MyString = new MyString;
$b = (string) $MyString;
var_dump($b); // string(Indoda)
```

Available casts include to string, integer, double, float, array, object and boolean. To determine the cast operator you require, you can use the following list.

type	cast operator
boolean	(bool)
integer	(int)
float	(float), (double) and (real)
array	(array)
object	(object)
string	(string)
NULL	(unset)

In addition PHP also has a few functions that can be used to obtain the value of variable as a certain type.

type	val* function
boolean	boolval()
integer	intval()
float	floatval()
double	doubleval() (simply an alias of floatval)

When implemented in a block of code they can be used in the following way:

```
$c = '10';
var_dump($c); // string(10)
var_dump(intval($c)); // int(10)
```

You can also use the `settype()` function and pass the intended output type as the second argument as a string.

```
$d = '10';
settype($d, 'int');
var_dump($d); // int(10)
```

This can accept one of either `'bool'`, `'int'`, `'float'`, `'string'`, `'array'`, `'object'` or `'null'`.

The `gettype()` companion function allows you to simply get the type of the supplied variable.

```
gettype($d); // integer
```

Typically, though, you would use the `is_*` set of functions to test the type of a variable. Again, there is a function for each type that PHP defines.

type	is_* function
array	is_array()
bool	is_bool()
float	is_float()
integer	is_int()
NULL	is_null()
object	is_object()
resource	is_resource()
string	is_string()

```
$e = 10;
var_dump(is_int($e)); // true
```

There are also some looser functions to make it easier to assess the contents of a variable in a broader sense. This means you can determine if a value is one of a collection of types.

type	is_* function
is_numeric()	integer, float (and double) or a string containing a numeric value
is_scalar()	integer, float, string, and boolean
is_callable()	the value of the variable can be treated as a function

```
$f = 10;
var_dump(is_numeric($f)); // true
```

As mentioned towards the beginning of this section, all of this is the beginning of the dynamic typing system PHP employs. The language parser also uses context to infer the type you want at run time. Where an operation is deemed to require an integer PHP will cast the value to an integer automatically. This makes sense where a number stored as a string is used in a calculation.

```
$g = '50';
$h = 50 + $g;
var_dump($h); // int(100)
```

PHP can see you are attempting to perform an addition with an integer (`50`) so it automatically casts `$a` to an integer (`50`) before attempting to perform the calculation. In this way the parser is actually performing an addition of `50` plus `50` resulting in `100`.

All of these attributes lead to PHP being a rather weak type system which can be a problem as it becomes difficult to ensure you are operating on the right type of data. There have been a number of attempts to bring stricter typing to PHP, and they were added in PHP 7. Enabling strict type hints is decided by the consuming code. Functions can use type hints to tell the PHP parser how to coerce arguments passed in to them.

Functions

Functions are a way to encapsulate a set of instructions into a reusable block. In PHP, functions may accept one or more arguments (sometimes referred to as parameters) and return a result. This takes the form of a name for the function and names for each of the arguments. Next, a body of the function lays out the steps required to produce the result with the supplied arguments.

Named Functions

Functions are usually defined as named functions in PHP—these are functions which are given a name at the point of definition. A simple function to add one to a supplied parameter can be expressed in the following way:

```
function add_one($x) {
    return $x + 1;
}
```

The arguments supplied to a function are substituted into the function's body and operated upon by the algorithm defined within. In the case of the `add_one()` function, there is only one parameter in the form of `$x`. When `add_one()` is called against a value the following steps are undertaken by the parser:

1. Call the function with an argument
   `add_one(3)`

2. Argument values are substituted into the function—`$x` becomes 3 meaning the body becomes
   `3 + 1`

3. Computation completed and an answer is calculated—`4`

4. Result returned from the function

Interestingly, this can easily be demonstrated with a nested call to `add_one()` in the form of `add_one(add_one(3))`. Essentially once this code is run the argument will have had `add_one()` applied to it twice in succession.

1. A call to the functions is made
   `add_one(add_one(3))`
2. The parser starts with the inner function first and substitutes its arguments into the body of the function
   `add_one(3 + 1)`
3. The computation is then worked upon giving
   `add_one(4)`
4. Now the parameter is passed into the outer function leaving the parser with
   `4 + 1`
5. Once again the calculation or work is performed inside the function to return a result—`5`

This illustrates the procedure of executing a function in the parser, but what about scoping?

Well, in PHP functions do not have access to variables declared outside the functions body. The only exceptions to the rules are variables passed into the function as arguments or those explicitly pulled in with the use of the `global` keyword.

To access a variable in the parent scope it must either be passed in as an argument or be declared as `global` in the function's body.

```
$a = 10;
function add_arg_to_global($x) {
   global $a;
   return $x + $a;
}
```

Although `$a` is not passed as an argument it is substituted into the function body by the use of the `global` keyword. This means if the function is applied to an argument of `1` the function body will be substituted to `10 + 1`.

```
echo add_arg_to_global(1); // 11
```

For the sake of completeness it is worth pointing out there are two further ways of doing this in PHP. You could add the variable to a superglobal such as `$GLOBALS`, `$_POST`, `$_SESSION`, etc. or you could use a closure, which will be discussed in an upcoming section of the book.

Superglobals are variables available in every scope in PHP. There are a total of nine superglobals defined by PHP and broadly speaking, you would only add values to two of them. When storing a value you wish to persist for the length of their session you would place the value in `$_SESSION`. Otherwise for it to last until the end of the current process you could write to `$GLOBALS`. Other superglobals include those concerned with request headers (`$_GET`, `$_POST`, `$_REQUEST`, `$_FILES` and `$_COOKIE`) and the environment (`$_SERVER` and `$_ENV`). While it is possible to change the values in these arrays it is generally advised against as this could cause unexpected results from scripts relying on these variables and their respective values.

In the past I have had cause to override `$_SERVER['DOCUMENT_ROOT']` in an `auto_prepend_file` for a mass virtual hosting setup. Another use I found is when setting the value of a cookie it will not be available until the next request from the user, so I will manually set it in the `$_COOKIE` array too to force it to be immediately available. However, this really is ill-advised.

While globals can give you an easy way of bringing values into a function body it is universally frowned upon—and with good reason! By relying on a global variable you **introduce state into your application**.

State should be avoided as it is difficult to recreate and leads to bugs in software. There will be more on this later, but for now just don't implement these schemes in your code!

At the end of the body (although it may appear before) it is usual practice to include a `return` statement. Those functions containing no return statement will emit a value of `null`. This can be achieved by either leaving the `return` keyword out altogether or by specifying `return;`. If you need to return more than one value from a function then you can return an array of values.

Finally, while it is possible to nest named functions within each other in PHP, they probably don't behave in the way you would expect. All named functions—no matter where they are defined—are interpreted to be at the parent scope. That is to say, functions nested inside another can be called from outside the containing function. They pollute the namespace too, so you cannot have a function with the same name as one declared in a nested function.

This means that you cannot have the code in Listing 3.1 and expect PHP to parse it.

Listing 3.1
```
01. function a() {
02.    function expr() {
03.       echo 'expression';
04.    }
05.    expr();
06. }
07.
08. function b() {
09.    function expr() {
10.       echo 'free';
11.    }
12.    expr();
13. }
```

As there are two functions defined with the name `expr()` PHP will throw a parse error regardless of the fact they appear nested inside another function.

Function Parameter Type Hinting

In functional programming it is common to use your languages compiler to help you write functions which accept values of a certain type and check your implementation before it even makes it to run time. In PHP this is difficult, as it is quite a loose type system and instead of a compiler PHP uses a runtime parser. As the code is not evaluated until it is run, errors cannot be machine detected.

There are some simple keywords you can employ to defend against the incorrect type being passed into a function.

- `array` specifies it must be an array
- A class name (`stdClass`)
- The name of an interface (`Traversable`)

Finally there is another type hint added in PHP 5.4 called `callable`, which denotes an argument which can be called like a function. In PHP. a callable can be any of the following:

- The name of an existing userland or PHP function as a string (`'substr'`)
- A class method can be specified as an array of two elements—first an instance and then the method name as a string (`[$object, 'myMethod']`)

- Static methods are similar, except instead of an instance you pass the class name as a string (`['MyClass', 'myMethod']`) or `MyClass::myMethod`
- Lambda functions and closures

If you value a stronger typing for PHP 5 (and you should), then Joe Watkins of Pthreads fame has been working on a PHP extension called Strict. This extension makes it possible to type hint for scalar types such as string or integer values when defining function parameters.

These type hints will trigger an exception if the incorrect type is passed into them. This allows you to rely on the correct type being passed into your routine. By default, PHP does not let you hint on scalar types at the moment.

Strict also brings a handy function using a so called lossless cast or throwing an exception where this is not possible. To determine the success of such a cast operation Strict checks if the conversion can be done without data or precision loss. So you would not be able to cast a float with decimals to an integer.

The only problem with the way Strict operates is default values cannot be specified for function arguments. This is due to Strict handling the arguments as classes behind the scenes. As you probably know it is not possible to supply an instance of a class as the default value of a function argument so this cannot be worked around.

Strict can provide a neat way around the limitations of PHPs type system. For functional programming this eases the need to check the input types of function arguments. The only alternative is to accept the value assuming the caller is passing in the correct type, and error if it is not. Hardly an elegant solution!

Advanced Function Calling

It is sometimes useful to be able to call a function programmatically by passing it an array of parameters. PHP has a couple of ways of doing this depending on the version of the language you're using.

Currently, the default approach is to use the `call_user_func_array()` function, but as we will see later variadics bring syntactic sugar to the exercise.

Quite possibly, the most common use of this technique is from inside a function when calling a second function with the same parameters or a subset of them. To illustrate this the following simple PHP log function outputs a terse debug message before calling the target function.

```
function log_and_call(callable $func_name) {
    $arguments = array_slice(func_get_args(), 1);
    echo $func_name . " called.\n";
    return call_user_func_array(
        $func_name,
        $arguments
    );
}
```

This function is very contrived and although it is not something I would employ in production it does, however, serve as a concise example. Now we can call it to see how it will react to input. Note the use of `array_slice()` to chop the first array element from `$arguments` as we don't need the name of the secondary function passed into the secondary function!

```
function hello($name) {
    return __FUNCTION__ . " $name";
}
echo log_and_call('hello', 'simon');
```

Outputs:

```
hello called
hello simon
```

Although this code may look complicated it is actually in fact quite simple; `log_and_call()` takes a function name followed by a 0..N list of parameters. Given these arguments it will echo the name of the function it is to call and execute the requested function. Arguments are passed from `log_and_call()` to the secondary function. Finally, the result of the function call is returned.

Like in PHP 5.6 it is possible to make use of variadics and the splat operator to greatly ease the readability of this kind of code.

In our previous examples we used `func_get_args()` to obtain an array of arguments. The unfortunate thing about this function is it returns all parameters regardless of whether you have assigned them to an argument variable already or not. This lead to the use of `array_slice()` to remove the first parameter in the previous example code.

Variadics make this process much easier and simpler with a slight syntax adjustment to your functions parameters. The last argument to your function can be prefixed with three consecutive dots. This instructs PHP to pass all subsequent parameters to your variadic variable as an array.

```
function sum3($a, $b, ...$xs) {
    return $a + $b + array_sum($xs);
}
```

We can then call this function with a set of parameters to see how the variadic behaves.

```
sum3(1, 2, 3, 4, 5, 6, 7, 8, 9, 10);
```

As `sum3()` is executed PHP will assign the first argument (1) to `$a` and the second (2) to `$b`. All subsequent arguments (3 through 10) will be assigned to the variadic `$xs`. This variable is designated as being variadic by the three preceding dots `...$xs`.

> You may be wondering why I have used the name xs for my variable—well it is a Haskell-esque convention to denote the variable contains a list of x. Just like natural English the 's' means it's a plural or many.
>
> So xs is a collection of values of type x where x could be `int`, `float`, etc.

Of course, this sample has no real application as you would normally dispense with the `$a` and `$b` variables and just use the variadic in `array_sum()`.

As previously mentioned the splat operator serves as an invaluable counterpart to the variadics. Also known as an unpacking operator it takes an array and turns the contents into an argument list for a function. The syntax is easy to remember given it is just the same as the variadic we examined.

This functionality can be shown in the following function call where PHP is essentially converting the supplied array $args into arguments against the sum() function defined earlier.

```
$args = [1, 2, 3, 4, 5, 6, 7, 8, 9, 10];
$r = sum3(...$args); // 55
```

Going back to the log_and_call() example it is possible to rewrite it using variadics and argument unpacking.

```
function log_and_call(callable $func_name, ...$arguments) {
    echo $func_name . " called.\n";
    return $func_name(...$arguments);
}
```

This code is significantly shorter and as a result quicker and easier to read. As the splat operator only collects the unassigned arguments, we're able to avoid slicing the $arguments array. Not to mention removing two function calls which are no longer necessary.

The splat or argument unpacking syntax added to PHP in version 5.6 allows for an array to be converted into function arguments. This array does not necessarily need to originate from a variadic or get_args() and can be an array you construct yourself. Variadics can be used to capture the arguments passed to a function as an array. It will pick up any arguments not already assigned to a named function parameter variable.

Lambda λ

Lambda functions are simply an extension of the basic PHP function idea. Essentially the lambda is a function which can be treated like a variable—it is a function without a formal identifier. By this I mean the function is not assigned a name at the time of definition. This trait is often known as a first class function, which means they can be passed as parameters to other functions, returned from a function assigned to a variable or placed in more complex data structures.

These functions are often referred to as lambda (λ) functions or anonymous functions interchangeably. To illustrate how this looks in PHP we'll reprise the add one function from earlier.

```
function($x) {
    return $x + 1;
};
```

Although this will compile, it will not actually do anything as we have no way of calling the function. Usually, a lambda function will be assigned to a variable or passed directly into another function as an argument.

When assigned to a variable the add one function can be called much like a standard PHP function although the variable is subject to the standard set of PHP scoping rules. Unlike a named function, a lambda function assigned to a variable is not immediately available from within other functions or class methods.

```
$add_one = function($x) {
    return $x + 1;
};
echo $add_one(4); // 5
```

The key difference between a standard named function and a lambda assigned to a variable is now it can be passed around, assigned to another variable, or even destroyed by calling `unset()` against `$add_one`.

```
unset($add_one);
```

In other words, it is possible to treat the function just like any other variable in PHP. All of these properties lead to the creation of higher order functions, which will be addressed in the next section.

If you have some experience with JavaScript, then this pattern will look very familiar as well.

```
var add_one = function($x) {
    return $x + 1;
};
```

In PHP you may have encountered lambda functions used for lazy loading, such as in a frameworks routing system. Another example can be found in the venerable `spl_autoload_register()` which takes a function as its first parameter:

```
$lambda_function = function($class_name) {
    include 'classes/' . $class_name . '.class.php';
};
spl_autoload_register($lambda_function);
```

As you can see, they can be assigned to variables, but equally, they can be defined directly in the parameter of the receiving function (in this case, `spl_autoload_register()`):

```
spl_autoload_register(function($class_name) {
    include 'classes/' . $class_name . '.class.php';
});
```

Anonymous functions are also known as lambda functions and they are declared with a formal name or identifier. They can be assigned to a variable, passed as an argument, or be returned from a function. One thing PHP will restrict you from doing is the serialization of anonymous functions as it will trigger a parsing error. There is at least one way round this with the help of Jeremy Lindblom's SuperClosure library[1], but it is not something many will need so it is left to you, dear reader, to dig in further should you find the need for it.

Formalized in Alonzo Church's papers, lambda functions are the basis of the lambda calculus. They also underpin all of the functional programming we will see in this book. Functional-style programming is not readily possible in languages without first class function support.

Forgive the hyperbole, but just about every piece of functional code ever written makes use of lambda functions, and they are an important building block to add to your tool kit and should be mastered before continuing.

Closures

Closures are an important feature of any functional language and have been deemed so useful that a lot of imperative languages now also support their use. PHP is no exception to this, with support for closures introduced in PHP 5.3.

Closures are a logical extension of the lambda function formalism by adding the concept of context to functions as they can be used to transport code and data around as a package. It could be considered that a closure represents a similar role in functional programming as objects perform in object-oriented programming. In fact, in PHP creating a closure actually returns an instance of the internal PHP `Closure` class.

[1] PHP SuperClosure—Version 2: https://github.com/jeremeamia/super_closure

More specifically, the context is a piece of information attached to the function at the point of definition. This information can be an PHP variable such as an array, a lambda function, scalars or objects. This is facilitated by the use keyword in PHP which pulls variables into a function from the current scope without having to pass them into the function as arguments—use ($add_value).

```
$add_value = 10;
$closure = function($param) use ($add_value) {
    return $param + $add_value;
};
echo $closure(2); // 12
echo $closure(60); // 70
```

It is important to note the value passed into the closure is set at the point of definition. This is unlike a global variable which can be changed anywhere and it will affect all code which later references it. A function operating on a global variable will return a different value if it is called again after the global variable is altered.

```
$my_global_var = 'sawubona';
function get_my_global_var() {
    global $my_global_var;
    return $my_global_var;
}
echo get_my_global_var(); // sawubona
$my_global_var = 'bye';
echo get_my_global_var(); // bye
```

If we were to do this with a closure then the value will be fixed at the point of defining our closure.

```
$my_global_var = 'sawubona';
$get_my_global_var = function() use ($my_global_var) {
    return $my_global_var;
};
echo $get_my_global_var(); // sawubona
$my_global_var = 'bye';
echo $get_my_global_var(); // sawubona
```

This succinctly demonstrates subsequent alterations of the value assigned to $my_global_var make no difference to the value encapsulated in our closure. This scoping is the most obvious difference between PHPs globals and constants as opposed to its closures.

The visual difference between a closure and any other PHP function is the use keyword which defines the variable or variables that will be pulled into and encapsulated by that closure. This is the only real difference and otherwise a closure looks just like any other lambda function.

```
$name = 'Haskell';
$my_first_closure = function() use ($name) {
    return "The first closure written by $name";
};
echo $my_first_closure();
// The first closure written by Haskell
```

In the previous example you will note the use keyword came into play and pulled in the $name variable. The function is then able to operate on the value of $name as if it were any other parameter passed to the function.

The same example with multiple variables added to the functions context via use would look like the following example.

```
$name = 'Haskell';
$surname = 'Curry';
$title = 'Mr.';
$my_first_closure = function() use ($name, $surname, $title) {
    return "The first closure written "
        . "by $title $name $surname";
};
echo $my_first_closure();
// The first closure written by Mr. Haskell Curry
```

Two new variables ($title and $surname) were added to the program and pulled into the functions context with the use keyword. This allowed all three variables to be used within the body of the closure, but of course you do not have to use all the variables pulled in. In the next example the $name variable has been added to the closures context, but it does not actually get consumed within the functions body.

```
$name = 'Haskell';
$surname = 'Curry';
$title = 'Mr.';
$my_first_closure = function() use ($name, $surname, $title) {
    return "The first closure written "
        . "by $title $surname";
};
echo $my_first_closure();
// The first closure written by Mr. Curry
```

Much like any other function a closure can also accept arguments and these are passed to it from within the first set of parentheses in the closures definition.

```
$salutation = 'Sawubona';
$my_closure = function($message) use ($salutation) {
    return "$salutation, $message";
};
echo $my_closure('I am hungry!');
// Sawubona, I am hungry!
echo $my_closure('please help me!');
// Sawubona, please help me!
```

Closures are useful for values you need access to on every call of the function and that will not change after the closure's definition. Commonly, it is implemented when you want to pass other closures or lambda functions into the closure you are defining.

Listing 3.2

```
01. $array = array(12345, 'abcde');
02. $lambda = function($value) {
03.     return md5($value);
04. };
05. $closure = function($value) use ($lambda) {
06.     return 'MD5 Hash: ' . $lambda($value);
07. };
08. $result = array_map($closure, $array);
09.
10. // array(
11. //     "MD5 Hash: 827ccb0eea8a706c4c34a16891f84e7b",
12. //     "MD5 Hash: ab56b4d92b40713acc5af89985d4b786"
13. // )
```

Here you can see a lambda function being pulled into a closure which is then called upon each element in $array using array_map() to create an MD5 hash for each value in the array.

Higher Order Functions

The term, higher order function, refers to functions which either accept another function as an argument or those returning a function as a value. Of course the same name applies to functions that do both as well. When a function accepts another function as a parameter like the venerable spl_autoload_register() it becomes a higher order function. You can create your own functions which accept other functions as parameters too.

This is most often used in PHP when you want to call a function against items in a list or to filter results as a predicate.

While this may be the norm you can pass the function for any purpose. Going back to the case of spl_autoload_register(), it is used as a sort of lazy loading and a simple function to define a reusable instruction set. By lazy loading I mean the code in the callback will not be executed unless it is required explicitly to answer an autoloading request. Additionally, if an earlier registered function matches, then this code will never run—a good thing!

Back to the original point and looking at an example of a function which accepts another function as an argument. We will start with a simple apply function which will accept a value and a function. Given these ingredients our apply function will execute the supplied function against the value parameter.

```
function apply(callable $func, $value) {
    return $func($value);
}
echo apply(
    function($x) { return $x + 1; },
    3
);
// 4
```

This could also be used against the $add_one lambda function we defined in the previous section.

```
echo apply($add_one, 3);
// 4
```

This is just the beginning of what is possible with this aspect of higher order functions and functional programming in general.

You have probably already encountered frameworks such as Silex, Bullet, and Slim that use lambda functions to handle the route/request process. These are anonymous functions in the wild being passed into higher order functions within the framework.

The other important property exhibited by higher order functions is the ability to return a function as a value and this allows for the creation of complex expressions (even more so with the help of closures). Keeping to simple functions and lambda functions it is possible to create a function which returns another function as a value.

Imagine you have an application supplied with hashes as either CRC32[2], MD5[3], SHA1[4] or SHA512[5]. Once the program has been given a hash it should then generate hashes using the same algorithm as the supplied hash. A simple, but error prone, way of doing this is to look at the length of hash and extrapolate what hashing algorithm was used.

Listing 3.3

```
01. function get_hashing_function($hash) {
02.    $hash_len = strlen((string) $hash);
03.    if(8 == $hash_len) {
04.        return function($x) { return dechex(crc32($x)); };
05.    } elseif(10 == $hash_len) {
06.        return function($x) { return crc32($x); };
07.    } elseif(32 == $hash_len) {
08.        return function($x) { return md5($x); };
09.    } elseif(40 == $hash_len) {
10.        return function($x) { return sha1($x); };
11.    } elseif(128 == $hash_len) {
12.        return function($x) { return hash('sha512', $x); };
13.    }
14. }
```

In the `get_hashing_function()` example (Listing 3.5), you can see there are two ways of detecting a CRC32 hash, this is because for historical reasons PHP's `crc32()` function returns an integer instead of a hexadecimal string like `md5()`. The `dechex()` function must be used to convert the integer to a hexadecimal representation. Otherwise this function is fairly straight forward; given a hash string it determines the length and then based on that, returns the appropriate hash function.

So given the hash `ef0f94622b0381c62cfb8fc5c6435f4c` it will calculate the length to be 32 characters and therefore make the assumption that `md5()` was used to generate the hash. Based on this knowledge it will give you a hash function back in return.

```
$supplied_hash = sha1('inja');
$hash_func = get_hashing_function($supplied_hash);
$a = ($supplied_hash === $hash_func('inja')); // true
$b = ('dog' === $hash_func('inja')); // false
```

[2] *Cyclic Redundancy Checksum polynomial of 32-bit lengths*
[3] *MD5 Message-Digest Algorithm*
[4] *US Secure Hash Algorithm 1*
[5] *US Secure Hash Algorithm 2*

While this functions serves to illustrate the concept at hand it is highly contrived and certainly not production ready. To simplify the example for higher order functions which return another function it is also possible to do the following.

```
function get_message() {
    return function() {
        echo 'sawubona';
    };
}
$message = get_message();
$message(); // sawubona
```

It is also possible to return an array of values from a function so you could return multiple functions in this way.

Higher order functions are at their most useful when using closures instead of just named and lambda functions, and they allow you to build powerful expressions. First, to keep it simple, the following example illustrates a function which returns a closure. This is denoted by the use keyword after the closures arguments and in this case it draws the value of $operator into the functions scope/context.

```
function create_maths_func($operator) {
    return function($a, $b) use ($operator) {
        return eval("echo $a $operator $b;");
    };
}
```

When passed a mathematical operator such as (+, -, /, * or %) create_maths_func() will return a closure which accepts two arguments. The closure will apply the supplied operator to the arguments ($a and $b) using PHP's eval() function.

```
$sum = create_maths_func('+');
echo $sum(10, 5); // 15

$sub = create_maths_func('-');
echo $sub(5, 1); // 4
echo $sub(10, 5); // 5
```

Closures can also be used to create more complex expressions such as repeating operations and introducing limit clauses. This is much more easily explained with a code example. To repeat a function call for number of times you can use a simple recursive function like the following code sample.

```
function repeat($times, $function, $state = []) {
    if($times > 0) {
        $state[] = $function($times);
        return repeat(--$times, $function, $state);
    }
    return $state;
}
```

I won't go into too much detail of the recursive nature of this function, as this is addressed in depth later in the book. For now, you can take my word it will call the supplied closure three times and return an array of the results. To add in some conditional logic, the `when()` function will take a condition and two callbacks. Based on the result of the condition it will either apply the first callback or the second.

```php
function when($condition, $do, $otherwise = null) {
    if($condition) return $do();
    elseif($otherwise) return $otherwise();
}
```

Essentially `when()` wraps an if/else statement up into a functional expression which can be applied in a sequence of function calls. In Listing 3.4 both `repeat()` and `when()` are combined to form a simple countdown.

Listing 3.4
```php
01. $res = repeat(3, function($i) {
02.     return when(
03.         $i == 1,
04.         function() use ($i) {
05.             return "$i. Final item";
06.         },
07.         function() use ($i) {
08.             return "$i. Counting down...";
09.         }
10.     );
11. });
12. // array (
13. //   0 => '3. Counting down...',
14. //   1 => '2. Counting down...',
15. //   2 => '1. Final item',
16. // )
```

This gives us a list of three items, but the same functions could easily be re-used elsewhere or applied to larger problems.

Instead of using control statements, functional programming makes use of higher order functions which form expressions. Higher order functions are those which take other functions as arguments and/or return a function.

See the following code sample for a very contrived example which exhibits some aspects of this paradigm. We are passing in a function as an argument and returning a function from `get_calculation()`. The function it returns will be executed against each item in the array by `array_map()`.

Listing 3.5 shows how functions can easily be reused and passed around to create richer algorithms. This is merely an extension of the functionality we saw earlier whilst exploring the `spl_autoload_register()` examples in the lambda functions section. It also serves as a timely reminder that if you're not careful, it is very easy to make a near unreadable mess with higher order functions in PHP!

Listing 3.5
```
01. $data = [1, 2, 3, 4, 5, 6, 7, 8, 9, 10];
02.
03. function get_calculation($rand_seed_fnc) {
04.     return (is_even($rand_seed_fnc())) ?
05.         function($value) {
06.             return $value * $value;
07.         } :
08.         function($value) use ($rand_seed_fnc) {
09.             return ($value * $value / $rand_seed_fnc()) + 10;
10.         };
11. }
12.
13. function is_even($value) {
14.     return ($value % 2 === 0);
15. }
16.
17. $rand_seed_fnc = function() {
18.     return rand();
19. };
20.
21. $results = array_map(get_calculation($rand_seed_fnc), $data);
```

You can also create more useful expressions with higher order functions with techniques of currying, composition, and partial function application—all of which will be addressed in the upcoming sections.

Function Objects

It is possible to treat a class instance as a function in PHP by calling any object implementing the __invoke() magic method as a function. This process is commonly known in the PHP world as a functor. In effect, the class instance becomes a closure when called in this way.

Listing 3.6
```
01. class SumFunctor
02. {
03.     public function __invoke($x, $y) {
04.         return $x + $y;
05.     }
06. }
07.
08. $SumFunctor = new SumFunctor;
09. echo $SumFunctor(5, 10); // 15
```

There are a number of reasons you might consider implementing your functions in this way, but the major advantages are that a closure becomes much easier to reuse and affords the ability to be more specific when type hinting. Of course, one limitation is a class can only have one function called in this manner. You can also access the class context, allowing for complex algorithms to be wrapped up into a neat package.

When the magic method is invoked it has the same scope as any class method meaning it can access any of the state contained in the object. In the case of the SumFunctor it would be possible to call another method to perform the calculation.

Listing 3.7
```
01. class SumFunctor
02. {
03.     public function __invoke($x, $y) {
04.         return $this->sum($x, $y);
05.     }
06.     public function sum($x, $y) {
07.         return $x + $y;
08.     }
09. }
10.
11. $SumFunctor = new SumFunctor;
12. echo $SumFunctor(5, 10); // 15
```

This approach has the advantage of being able to access the same `sum()` method using standard object access or via the `__invoke()` magic method. Calling `__invoke()` directly using object access is pretty ugly and should be avoided where possible in deference to more readable method names.

```
$SumFunctor = new SumFunctor;
echo $SumFunctor->sum(5, 10); // 15
```

```
// Yuck!
echo $SumFunctor->__invoke(5, 10); // 15
```

Existing class instances may also share their context with a closure by using the `Closure::bind` and `Closure::bindTo` methods. This allows you to take an existing class scope and share it with a closure. Both `bindTo` and `bind` accept a closure as a parameter and return a new closure with access to the associated class' scope.

Listing 3.8
```
01. class StringContainer
02. {
03.     public $value = 'My name is ';
04. }
05.
06. $echo_name = function($name) {
07.     echo $this->value . $name;
08. };
09.
10. $SC = new StringContainer;
11. $bound_echo_name = $echo_name->bindTo($SC);
12. $bound_echo_name('Simon'); // My name is Simon
```

If you also need to be able to access protected and private members of the class you can specify the scope as a second parameter for bindTo by either supplying a class instance or the class name as a string.

Listing 3.9
```
01. class Greeting extends StringContainer
02. {
03.     private $greeting = 'Sakubona. ';
04. }
05.
06. $echo_greeting = function($name) {
07.     echo $this->greeting . $this->value . $name;
08. };
09.
10. $G = new Greeting;
11. $bound_echo_greeting = $echo_greeting->bindTo($G, $G);
12. $bound_echo_greeting('Simon'); // Sakubona. My name is Simon
```

Using bind is very similar except it is a static method so you must pass the closure into it allowing for shorter code. We can rewrite the previous example using bind in the following manner:

```
$G = new Greeting;
$bound_echo_greeting = Closure::bind(
    function($name) {
        echo $this->greeting . $this->value . $name;
    },
    $G, $G
);
$bound_echo_greeting('Simon');
```

Defining the closure right inside the call to bind allows us to forgo assigning it to an interim variable such as $echo_greeting in the previous code sample.

Unlike when using __invoke() inside a class it is also possible to bind more than one closure to the instances scope. Conversely, using a functor allows you to make use of PHP's namespace aliasing.

```
use MyFunctionObject as M;
$M = new M;
```

This is a small secondary benefit and PHP 5.6 merged a patch to facilitate aliasing standard functions using PHP's namespace syntax too.

There are at least two downfalls of function objects however and the first of which is most annoying. You cannot currently call the function inline without creating the instance first like so:

```
$f = new F;
echo $f();
```

Hopefully, something along the lines of the following code will be added to PHP to facilitate the easier access style of doing:

```
echo (new F)();
```

Additionally function objects can be frowned upon as they are not self-documenting. Every __invoke() API can be different making predictable use difficult. In my research most IDEs are not able to give parameter hints for the function objects either.

It should be noted this functionality is not actually a functor as defined by category theory and a more accurate computing-based term would be a function object. In category theory, a functor is a mapping between two categories where the structure of the category being mapped is preserved.

Having said that, the term functor is used to describe a number of differing techniques across languages, and PHP is siding with C++ in this respect.

Namespacing

PHP acquired namespaces in version 5.3 and they have almost universally replaced the older PEAR style of namespacing (underscores replaced directory separators so /Vendor/MyClass.php became Vendor_MyClass). While the syntax is much maligned by many (and for good reason) it is great to finally have namespaced code in PHP. Now most projects only use object oriented code, so it is little known functions can also be namespaced.

It is pretty much the same syntax as you will find on classes where the top of the file declares a namespace and this namespace is then applied to the whole class container as described in Listing 3.9.

Listing 3.9
```
01. namespace Treffynnon {
02. class MyNamespacedClass {
03.    function __toString() {
04.        echo __CLASS__;
05.    }
06. }
07.
08. // then when calling from elsewhere
09. $inst = new \Treffynnon\MyNamespacedClass;
```

Functions, on the other hand, have no bounding container to group them like the methods do in Listing 3.2 with their wrapping class (MyNamespacedClass). This is where namespaces can actually be used to wrap our functions directly.

The namespace clause can be used with wrapping braces around the functionality that should be namespaced with Listing 3.10.

Listing 3.10
```
01. <?php
02. namespace Treffynnon\File {
03.    function get($path) {
04.        if(is_readable($path)) {
05.            return file_get_contents($path);
06.        }
07.    }
08. }
09. namespace Treffynnon\Parse {
10.    function csv($string) {
11.        return str_getcsv($string);
12.    }
13. }
```

Again, calling these functions is much like instantiating a namespaced class or calling methods within it. You simply include a use statement to indicate the namespace you wish to pull in.

```
use \Treffynnon\File as F,
    \Treffynnon\Parse as P;

$csv_array = P\csv(F\get(__FILE__));
```

This is a simple way of writing functional code which will not complain when you define two functions with the same name. Unfortunately, that is all it can do and if you were hoping for autoloading, then you will be understandably upset. There are ways around this, but they are not very nice and unrelated to namespacing so they exist in the *Hazards of Functional Programming in PHP chapter.*

Recursion

Basics

To eliminate flow control statements such as `for`, `foreach`, and `while` in your programs, you can create loops using recursion. This is a process of repeatedly calling a function from within itself until a predetermined cut-off is reached.

A very common use of recursion in web programming revolves around printing site menu structures from content management systems, and it is also a good fit for working through file system directory trees.

```
$array = ['i', 'k', 'h', 'a', 'n', 'd', 'a'];
function concat($array, $index = 0, $result = '') {
    return (array_key_exists($index, $array))
        ? concat($array, $index + 1, $result . $array[$index])
        : $result;
}
echo concat($array); // ikhanda
```

In the example above, the function recursively calls itself until it reaches the end of the array. Along the way, it joins each element of the array together.

On each iteration, the code first determines if the requested array index exists, and if it does, then it recursively calls itself (`concat()`), adds one to the index `$index`, and concatenates the current array element onto the end of the string `$result`. When it hits the end of the array, it will return the value of `$result`, and the recursion will end.

You would never actually concatenate a string in this way, but it serves as a simple illustration of performing actions without variable assignment statements in tandem with recursive "looping".

Tail Call Recursion

Most recursive functions in PHP are written without tail call recursive, but it can be superior in some cases.

Recursion causes the compiler to wait for a result from the called function before it can return a result of its own. On the other hand, tail call recursion allows the compiler to make optimizations to increase speed and reduce resource usage. Unfortunately, PHP does not take advantage of this, but it is still a good technique to master as in some cases, it can make the code clearer.

A simple example to show the two different styles with the more common recursive form first:

```
function recursive_sum($x) {
    return ($x == 1)
        ? $x
        : $x + recursive_sum($x - 1);
}
```

The parser will have to process all the recursive calls to `recursive_sum()` before it can finally add the result to `$x`. Tail call recursion implementing the same functionality would look like the following function:

```
function tail_sum($x, $running_total = 0) {
   return ($x == 0)
      ? $running_total
      : tail_sum($x - 1, $running_total + $x);
}
```

`tail_sum()` does not have the same problem as each iteration performs the calculation directly in line.

Unfortunately, as previously mentioned, PHP—much like Python—does not take advantage of the performance opportunities tail call recursion provides.

Mutual Recursion

So far, we have covered what is known as direct recursion—where a function calls itself to create the loop. For example, if function `x()` calls `x()` itself, then it is direct recursion.

You can also implement indirect recursion (sometimes known as mutual recursion by extension) to produce a loop by creating a function, which later calls the original function again. This is where function `x()` calls function `y()`, which subsequently calls `x()` again, and the loop repeats itself from there.

Recursive Lambdas

On the face of it lambdas do not appear to be able to call themselves, but depending on the version of PHP you are running there are a few relatively simple ways of doing it.

The most obvious way is to pass the variable; a lambda is assigned to into itself with the `use` keyword. Seems simple and you have probably already thought of using it this way, but having tried it you may well be disappointed by a nondescript PHP error.

Surprisingly, the variable must actually be passed by reference for the operation to have any chance of succeeding. This is because at the point the variable is fed into the lambda it has not been defined (the lambda that is) and its value, therefore, is still `null`. When the variable is passed by reference it does not matter its value is `null` because it will be updated with a reference to the lambda function once the parser finishes executing its definition.

```
$f = function($x = 0) use (&$f) {
   return ($x < 10)
      ? $f($x + 1)
      : $x;
};
$a = $f(); // 10
```

While passing by reference avoids the issue, it also breaks the standard definition of an anonymous function. If you were to later modify a variable passed by reference, it would change inside the lambda too. This is counter intuitive as this is not how lambdas work by default and you are also allowing global mutable state into your application.

If you have used a function object then it gets even easier as `$this` is there to help you make the recursive calls without any by-reference nastiness. The next code sample is solving the same problem as the previous code example, but with a function object instead.

```
class RecursiveFunctionObject {
   public function __invoke($x = 0) {
      return ($x < 10)
         ? $this->__invoke($x + 1)
         : $x;
   }
}
$RFA = new RecursiveFunctionObject;
$b = $RFA(); // 10
```

While the code is longer in this case, it does remove the rather horrible after taste left behind by the shared mutable state introduced by the `use` keyword.

The need to recurse a lambda crops up rarely in my experience and there are generally other options, but when you need it these tricks can really help.

Don't Blow the Stack

Recursive loops are powerful, but there are a few things to be mindful of when implementing them in your code. If you fail to include an exit condition, or if you choose one that is overly broad, you run the risk of unexpected behavior. Usually, this manifests itself as a stack overflow exception.

The compiler will keep looping until something stops it, so if you or the time out protections do not stop it, the final limitation is the machine's physical resources. In this case, it will most likely be the memory limitations that you come up against first.

Bear in mind all calls, parameters, and variable assignments in a recursive call have an impact on the amount of memory consumed. For example, your process will run out of memory more quickly when you have debugging code inside of it!

Map, Reduce, and Filter

Map/reduce provides a simple way to create elegant code solutions to complex list processing operations, and it has proven useful for high-availability, large-scale processing. You may have heard of Hadoop, CouchDB, and similar NoSQL solutions implementing map/reduce—not to mention Google's indexing algorithm. Using `array_map()` and `array_reduce()`, it is also possible to exploit these techniques with PHP.

Map

Map iterates over a set of data to produce a new list of values by applying a function to each item in the list. Most `for` and `foreach` loops can easily be replaced with a call to `array_map()`. The key difference is it separates the computational function from the loop itself.

Of course, this easily lends itself to code re-use where you may need to apply the same operation to a list in a different context.

On the other hand, in PHP at least, it is slightly slower to use `array_map()` than employing `foreach`, but unless you are the kind of developer to fret over micro-optimizations, the difference is negligible.

```
function times_two($val) { return $val * 2; }
$array = [1, 2, 3, 4, 5];
$results = array_map('times_two', $array);
// array(2, 4, 6, 8, 10)
```

An interesting thought for you now—the list could contain functions and not just primitive values. You could use `array_map()` to execute all the functions contained in an array and return all their values, for example.

Reduce

Reduce, on the other hand, loops over a list to collapse or combine the values therein into one final value by applying the same processing function to each value in the list. This operation is sometimes known as a fold function, and the PHP `array_reduce()` function can be considered analogous to a left fold.

In the following reduce example, you can see it operates on a list of integers and adds each element to a total. This is an iterative process which works upon one element in the array at a time.

```
function sum($result, $val) {
    return $result + $val;
}
$array = [1, 2, 3, 4, 5];
$sum = array_reduce($array, 'sum', 0);
// 15
```

In Tandem

Of course, these two techniques can be combined to great effect. If you were to have a set containing a list of documents, you could use a mapping function to iterate through each one and calculate its file size on disk. In addition, it would be great to know the total file size so you could use a reduce function to iterate over the file sizes and sum them up, reusing the `sum()` function created above.

```
function get_filesize($path) {
    return filesize($path);
}
$total = array_reduce(
    array_map('get_filesize', $array_of_file_paths),
    'sum',
    0
);
```

Here you have seen `array_reduce()` directly working upon the array result returned by `array_map()`. It is a very simple example, but you can use these two operations to easily work through lists, large or small.

You may have noticed a highly irritating fact about PHP's implementation of these two little functions—they don't maintain the same parameter order! Reduce accepts the collection (or array) first and then the callback function, whereas map is the opposite way around.

Gimme the Keys!

The difficulty with both map and reduce in PHP is there is no access to the array key. The only real way to remedy this is to write your own implementation. There is another function which is very similar to map called `array_walk()`. While this does supply the key, it also mutates the array it is working on—yuck!

So the logical response is to wrap `array_walk()` in a custom function we will call `map2()`. This function ensures a copy of the array is fed to `array_walk()` so the state of the array passed into it is not mutated as calling `array_walk()` directly would.

As PHP passes arrays by value and not reference the copy of the array is automatically created for us simply by wrapping `array_walk()` in another function. This should mean that `map2()` is actually a very simple enhancement to create.

Well not so fast, the code below includes a closure which performs two extra actions. The first item of business is to fix the order the key and value are injected into the map2() callback function. On top of this, it handles the translation of the return clause in map2()s to an array_walk() value assignment via reference.

```
function map2(array $list, callable $func) {
    array_walk($list, function(&$value, $key) use ($func) {
        $value = $func($key, $value);
    });
    return $list;
}
```

This makes the callback function behave much more like an array_map() callback and in a more functional way. You could also use recursion to solve this problem:

```
function map2(array $list, callable $func, $carry = []) {
    if($list) {
        $key = reset(array_keys($list));
        $value = reset($list);
        $carry[$key] = call_user_func($func, $key, $value);
        return map2(array_splice($list, 1), $func, $carry);
    }
    return $carry;
}
```

Another recursive method making use of a tracking/carry variable to maintain the state is implemented above. Note that all three methods are functionally equivalent and produce the same result when given the same values as arguments.

Listing 3.12
```
01. function map2(array $list, callable $func) {
02.     $key = reset(array_keys($list));
03.     $return = [
04.         $key => $func($key, reset($list))
05.     ];
06.
07.     if($new_list = array_splice($list, 1)) {
08.         return array_merge(
09.             $return,
10.             map2($new_list, $func)
11.         );
12.     }
13.
14.     return $return;
15. }
```

These functions can then be used much like `array_map()` to apply a function to each item in an array, but the `$func` will be passed both the key and the value.

```
$data = [
    'one'   => 'Pail',
    'two'   => 'Bucket',
    'three' => 'Hod',
];
$out = map2($data, function($key, $value) {
    return "$key: " . strtoupper($value);
});
```

If you call `var_dump($out)` you see:

```
array(3) {
  'one' =>
  string(9) "one: PAIL"
  'two' =>
  string(11) "two: BUCKET"
  'three' =>
  string(10) "three: HOD"
}
```

It is also possible to do the same with `array_reduce()` by making use of a closure to handle the requirement for keys. We can iterate over the keys and then obtain the value later using the key inside `$fx`.

```
function map2(array $list, callable $func) {
    array_walk($list, function(&$value, $key) use ($func) {
        $value = $func($key, $value);
    });
    return $list;
}
```

Flat Map

When we deal with mapping over lists it is quite common that we will want to apply a function that will return an array. The final result we want though is just a simple one dimensional array rather than the two dimensional array we would be returned by default.

Let us start with an example of the problem so you can easily see where this might happen in your code.

```
array_map(function($x) {
    return explode(' ', $x);
}, ['1 2 3', '4', '5', '6 7 8']);
// [['1', '2', '3'], ['4'], ['5'], ['6', '7', '8']]
```

We actually want a simple one dimensional list to be returned and this is where our friend `flat_map()` comes into play.

```
flat_map(function($x) {
    return explode(' ', $x);
}, ['1 2 3', '4', '5', '6 7 8']);
// ['1', '2', '3', '4', '5', '6', '7', '8']
```

In PHP flat_map() can be defined using an array_reduce() to merge the results of each function application into the first dimension. It is worth noting that a flat_map() does not flatten all dimensions—just the second into the first—so if you have a deeply nested array it will not affect the lower dimensions. If you need this then use flatten() (defined later in the book) to reduce the nesting after using array_map() to apply the function.

```php
function flat_map(callable $func, $data) {
    $f = function($acc, $x) use ($func) {
        return array_merge($acc, $func($x));
    };
    return array_reduce($data, $f, []);
}
```

Flat map is a very common operation in functional programming and most languages have a specialised flat map function to help you work through this problem. It is very handy that the same functionality can be replicated in PHP with a quite a simple set of code.

Filter

With the help of filtering, you can return a result set from a list of values by applying a callback function known as a predicate to each item in the list. The predicate will return either a Boolean false to remove the record, or true to keep the list item in the result set. While this may sound a little complicated, in practice, it makes cleaning lists a breeze.

```php
function filter_callback($val) {
    return ($val % 2 === 0);
}

$evens = array_filter(
    array(1, 2, 3, 4, 5),
    'filter_callback'
);
// array(2, 4);
```

In the preceding example, we are applying a filter callback to a simple list of integers. The callback itself checks if the supplied number is cleanly divisible by two, which is a simple way of detecting if the value is an even or an odd number.

array_filter() is then used to iterate over the array of integers and apply the callback to each value therein. This results in a new array being returned that contains only the even numbers, being two and four in this case.

Memoization

The process of result caching can help to speed up expensive operations by returning a pre-chewed set of data. Fetching the values from a cache allows an application to skip the slow running code and still return the correct results. The secret sauce of PHP's memoization is the `static` keyword, which effectively pins a variable to a resource in memory. Any time the resource is updated in the same PHP process, the new value is recalled on the next invocation of the function.

```
function memoized_expensive_data() {
    static $array = [];
    return empty($array)
        ? $array = get_some_really_expensive_data()
        : $array;
}
```

This operation can be simplified by using the `F\memoize()` function of the functional-php library (discussed more in-depth later):

```
use Functional as F;

$callback_function = function($arg) {
    return get_some_really_expensive_data($arg);
};
$result = F\memoize($callback_function, array('php'));
```

A good example of where this might be useful is in caching the parsing of large documents into a hash or limiting calls to a database for a widely-reused function.

Generators

When working with a large dataset it becomes inefficient to have the entirety of it loaded in memory such as with an array for example. To ease this process PHP added the generator syntax[6] in version 5.5, which is a simplified way of creating a PHP iterator.

If we look at the sum example running through this book we can write our own version of `array_sum()` that accepts a generator instead of an array. This function will work its way through the values contained in the generator and sum them all together.

```
function sum2($values) {
    $total = 0;
    foreach($values as $i) {
        $total += $i;
    }
    return $total;
}
```

You will immediately note nothing special appears to be going on here and you would be correct. It is simply a `foreach` loop adding each value (`$i`) to the `$total` variable. You could pass an array into this function and it would work just as well. The trick is in how `$values` is populated and not how it is consumed.

---

[6]   PHP Generators: http://php.net/language.generators

To generate some values it is necessary to write a range function which produces a generator instead of an array. This function will look very familiar too with one simple exception that makes this a generator.

```
function range2($start, $end) {
  for($i = $start; $i <= $end; $i += 1) {
    yield $i;
  }
}
```

Note the `yield` keyword inside the for loop—the only real deviation from any array based range function you may write. Now we have our two base functions we can call them together to see how they work.

```
echo sum2(range2(1, 10));
// 55
```

A more complex and useful example of a generator is one which makes file reading more efficient. This can be used to work on large files without reaching memory limits or exceeding an execution timeout.

The beauty of using a generator in this way is you create a more abstract interface for operating on a file. The consuming code does not need to even know its operating on a file; it just knows it has an iterator it needs to work through. This means you could use the functions from your library you have written to work with arrays all without changing their implementation to handle file transformations.

This could also be achieved with PHP's `file()` function which reads an entire file as an array, but it would not suit large files as it would have memory consumption implications.

Chapter

Helpful Libraries

"We can only see a short distance ahead, but we can see plenty
there that needs to be done."

—Alan Turing (Mathematician and Computer Scientist,
1912–1954)

Now that you have seen some techniques for manipulating data in a functional way, you are probably wondering which primitives and higher order functions PHP has to offer in the default installation. Unfortunately, the answer is not many, although this constantly changing as the language evolves. To help fill this void, Lars Strojny has created a PECL extension called functional-php[1]. If you are unable to install PECL extensions on your host, then there is a pure PHP userland version of the library available.

Many, if not all, of the functions are inspired by implementations of functional primitives in other languages such as JavaScript and Scala. Unfortunately, at this stage there is no implementation of any sorting functionality in the extension or library, but it is on the road map for the project.

Not only does functional-php have handy primitives, but it also unifies the interface for operating on lists. All functions have the same order of parameters, so no more hassle remembering whether it is the collection or callback which comes first! Another very handy feature is in addition to arrays, its functions can operate on any object that implements PHP's Traversable interface.

[1]   functional-php: https://github.com/lstrojny/functional-php

It is important to try to keep the API consistent with your own code and when importing other functional libraries to facilitate easier future maintenance.

Additionally, there is the Underscore.php[2] library written by Brian Haveri, which is a pure PHP set of functional primitives covering a lot of the same ground as functional-php. There are one or two additional features such as `__::sortBy` and `__::compose()`, so you may want to use the two projects in tandem. Another similar library includes Nicolò Martini's Functionals[3].

As previously mentioned in the partial function application section, React/Partial[4] is a very handy library to have available to your projects for partial function application syntactic sugar.

Library Installation

The main library used throughout the following code samples is functional-php, and it can either be installed as a PHP/PECL extension or as a userland PHP library. If you have the option, then I would suggest the extension route, but if you can't build or install extensions on your server, then you can use the library. For initial playing around, you may find it easier to opt for the library route as well. If you are following along on a Windows machine, then install it as a library.

If you have chosen to install it as a library rather than an extension, please skip to the "Other PHP Libraries" section heading below.

functional-php

The functional-php extension must be built from source as the PECL releases are old and missing the latest features. The first thing to do is to download a ZIP file of the source from GitHub[5]. Extract the ZIP file to a suitable temporary folder somewhere, and then change directories into it. From inside the functional-php projects root folder, execute the following commands:

```
phpize
./configure
make
sudo make install
```

Once the extension is built using any of the aforementioned methods, you will also need to enable it in the `php.ini` file by adding the line:

```
extension=functional.so
```

It should be noted here if you are using this extension with a website rather than on the PHP CLI, then you will need to restart your web server for the new PHP configuration to take effect.

> **Note:** *You should remove the functional-php line from the* `composer.json` *requirements described in the next section before installing the dependencies if you have already installed functional-php via the extension method described above. If you fail to do this, the userland PHP library version will still be installed, though it will be ignored harmlessly in deference to the PHP extension.*

---

[2] Underscore.php: *http://brianhaveri.github.com/Underscore.php/*
[3] nicmart/Functionals: *https://github.com/nicmart/Functionals*
[4] React/Partial: *https://github.com/reactphp/partial*
[5] Functional PHP ZIP file: *https://github.com/lstrojny/functional-php/archive/master.zip*

Other PHP Libraries

With the exception of functional-php, all the aforementioned libraries are supplied as userland PHP code allowing them to be installed via the usual methods such as downloading a tarball. However, with the help of the Composer dependency management system and the Packagist repository, you can make the process much simpler.

To get started, you will need to install Composer per the instructions in *PHP Libraries in Chapter 1*.

```
curl -s http://getcomposer.org/installer | php
```

Also in the base folder of the application, you should define a JSON object in the composer.json file to configure the dependencies of your project. To make this process quicker and easier, see Listing 4.1 which contains the full composer.json requirements file for all the aforementioned libraries. Should you not wish to install a library, you can simply remove it from the list. For more information on the requirements file format, please see the Composer documentation[6].

Listing 4.1
```
01. {
02.   "repositories": [
03.     {
04.       "type": "package",
05.       "package": {
06.         "name": "brianhaveri/Underscore.php",
07.         "version": "dev-master",
08.         "dist": {
09.           "url": "https://github.com/brianhaveri/Underscore.php/archive/master.zip",
10.           "type": "zip"
11.         },
12.         "autoload": {
13.           "classmap": ["underscore.php"]
14.         }
15.       }
16.     }
17.   ],
18.   "require": {
19.     "react/partial": "~2.0",
20.     "nicmart/functionals": "dev-master",
21.     "brianhaveri/Underscore.php": "dev-master",
22.     "lstrojny/functional-php": "dev-master",
23.     "phpoption/phpoption": "1.*",
24.     "nikic/iter": "1.*"
25.   }
26. }
```

Once you have decided which libraries to install, and have amended your composer.json file appropriately, you can install them with a single command:

```
composer install
```

Should a project you depend upon be updated with changes at a later date, you can simply call update with:

```
composer update
```

[6]   Composer documentation: http://getcomposer.org/doc/

Now, in your project's bootstrap or index file, you can include all of the Composer/Packagist supplied dependencies by simply adding this line of PHP code:

```
require 'vendor/autoload.php';
```

If you are using version control (and you should be), then you will want to remember to ignore/exclude `composer.phar`, and the `vendor` directory before committing.

The iter Library

Generators and iterators are very handy features of PHP, but like most of the features we have studied there are some rough edges. The userland `iter` library helps to make their usage simpler and cleaner. The library can be installed as a dependency with composer much like the other libraries we have reviewed here. The main benefit it provides is a set of functions which can be universally applied to all PHP iterables, arrays, traversables, and aggregates. These include implementations of map, reduce, and range which we have seen previously. The exception here is they can be applied everywhere and to all PHP collections.

To make the code more efficient all access is completed via generators which allows the library to be lazy. By this I mean it will only actually complete the work when, and only when, it is needed for the continued execution of the program. This is the opposite of eager loading where as much work is done up front as possible, even if the result may not actually be used in this context.

So you get the benefit of a better API and improved overall performance. To keep it simple we will start with an example we have seen a few times already: summing up a range of integers.

```
use iter, iter\fn;
$r = iter\range(1, 10);
$sum = iter\reduce(fn\operator('+'), $r); // 55
```

It can also be used in more complicated functional code with good results. If you have to deal with an array of items and you cannot be sure they are all of the same type then the `iter\takeWhile` function can really help.

```
$values = [1, 2, 3, 4, 'ten', 'twenty'];
$sum = iter\reduce(
    fn\operator('+'),
    iter\takeWhile(function($a) {
        return is_int($a);
    }, $values)
); // 10
```

This library is a very handy replacement for many of PHP's list/iterable access functions. Alongside functional-php it can create a very useful toolkit of primitives.

As this library is based upon generators the iterables are not currently rewindable by default. To work around this the library has in-built support for iterator conversion to rewindables.

```
use iter, iter\fn;
$res = iter\callRewindable(
    'iter\\map',
    fn\operator('*', 3),
    [1, 2, 3]
); // [3, 6, 9]
```

Generators from the iter library are already bestowed with a rewindable variant under the iter\rewindable namespace. Any function such as map, reduce, etc. from the iter library can be called this way for rewindable functionality.

```
$res = iter\rewindable\map(
    fn\operator('*'),
    [1, 2, 3]
); // [3, 6, 9]
```

The functions this library provides are very useful when dealing with lists in PHP 5.5 and above where generators are supported. They are predictable with the callback function always coming first where applicable. It is a very well thought out library which replaces core PHP functions with a much neater interface.

Where possible I would recommend you add it as a dependency to all your applications be they functional or not. Then simply take a list of any type and apply your will to it just as we would wish PHP's in-built functions to do.

Chapter

5

HHVM's Hack

> *"Never had any mathematical conversations with anybody because there was nobody else in my field."*
>
> —Alonzo Church (Mathematician and Logician, 1903–1995)

Facebook has been using PHP for years, but as the site's membership grew so did its load times. In a bid to speed up PHP they wrote an internal-use-only transpiler that could convert a small subset of PHP to a C program. This resulted in much faster load times, but was cumbersome to use and required specialist internal knowledge to run correctly. As time wore on this became less and less viable and the code started to take longer to compile. Eventually a new project was started which would go on to be called HipHop Virtual Machine or HHVM for short. It is a just-in-time parser which creates an efficient cached representation of your program as it is executed. To obtain the best performance this cache must be warmed by running the target code a number of times to allow HHVM to get the most optimal picture of your code. It is worth noting the JIT aspect does not enhance performance on the command line as a new cache is used on every invocation.

Alongside this new and faster runtime Facebook also needed a few features to be added to the language. This has grown to become the Hack language. The languages are essentially the same with Hack being a fork of PHP, albeit on its own runtime.

To notify the compiler you are using Hack instead of PHP you simply use `<?hh` as the opening tag instead of `<?php`. HHVM will see this tag and then parse the code as Hack instead of straight PHP. Inside these tags you can perform operations just like you would with PHP, but benefit from improved JITing as you refactor the code slowly to Hack. There are some things PHP supports which HHVM has deliberately omitted as their actual implementations is in the wilds of PHP are limited. To ensure they achieve a reasonable parity, Facebook has chosen a number of open source projects to compile unit tests against.

This involved picking the top few PHP projects on GitHub with a good test suite. They then run these tests against their HHVM builds to see where they fail. Having identified areas where support is lacking they work through the failed tests until they are solved. The idea is to achieve parity with PHP to make the runtime easier to adopt for existing projects and PHP shops.

This desire to match PHP even led the Facebook crew to create the beginnings of a language specification. This is simply a document detailing what the language should do and its required core library. After preparing it they then open sourced it for the PHP team to maintain.

This highlights one aspect of PHP that differentiates it from many other languages such as Python or Ruby. Instead of having a specification to work from when the PHP runtime was written they (well, OK, just Rasmus in the very beginning) simply implemented features. I imagine this is because it was quicker, easier, and presumably no one thought other implementations of the language (such as HHVM) would be written. Well, fast forward a number of years and we have HHVM, Zephir, HippyVM and Quercus (on the Java Virtual Machine or JVM).

This is a new thing for PHP to have such a high profile alternative, but in the case of Python it is something they are used to and even demand. There the language is implemented as IronPython (.NET), Jython (JVM) and CPython (C) giving more diverse options to the developer. The Zend Engine for PHP on the other hand, can be considered the de facto reference implementation of the language and any other runtime would have to emulate its quirks.

Back to the Hack language itself though it can be considered an extension of the PHP language in its own right. That said, it contains some very useful features which enrich the base of PHP dramatically. Oh, and Hack is written in OCaml—a functional (amongst other paradigms) programming language.

Types

One of the weakest parts of PHP 5, in my opinion, is the type system and Hack goes a long way to address this with its extensions to the type system. In PHP there is very little to allow the creation of types unless you want to box values in wrapping classes—an arduous task.

In Hack however, you can use type aliases to create new types which can then be referenced throughout your code. This better support greatly eases the laborious task of code maintenance. It also makes it easier to reason about the code you produce as you are writing new features in an application.

First, though, let us step back to the basics and review the core in-built types Hack provides. These are the same types as PHP defines itself for the most part.One key difference though is scalar types (int, string, etc) can be hinted in function arguments. On top of this, the return type can also be defined allowing you to reason further about the code and the parser to report on type mismatches. As discussed previously this helps to eliminate a whole class of bugs.

While PHP does have types they are not easily hinted and variables can change type at any time. This makes it difficult to write code which expects a certain type to operate on. Prior to PHP 7, you could either use some kind of type testing switch statement or cast to the type you expect hoping the value still makes sense. This is an asset to PHP as it makes the language freer and therefore easier to learn. When you want to write abstracted code though it becomes a hindrance.

This is where Hack lang's type system can help. It is possible to avoid declaring types as Hack will infer the type from the value you are assigning. If an integer is assigned at declaration, then the resulting type of the variable will automatically be `int`. This behavior is much the same as PHP until it comes to type hinting.

A function could be defined as accepting only an integer for its first parameter as follows, which also states it will return an `int`.

```
function x2(int $a):int {
    return $a * 2;
}
```

Here you can see the parameter `$a` has been specified as an integer. By default, Hack will attempt to cast any non-`int` values to integers before passing the value into the function. This can lead to some unexpected behavior.

You can set how strict you want the Hack parser to be by placing a comment after the opening `<?hh` tag. This allows you to run various code at various levels of strictness, which is not a good thing. This can lead to confusion and it is annoying to have to add the comment all the time. On the flip side it makes it possible to drop down to a less strict mode if necessary.

To be able to call PHP code from Hack you must not use `strict` mode in the calling file for example. This is because strict requires code to have types defined and be written in Hack lang. Other reasons this can be handy is if there is a problem with Hack's type checker or when calling incorrectly typed code. Strict is the most stringent of all the modes and it is the one I recommend coding to. It requires all code to be correctly annotated with types or it will fail to parse the code. As all code requires types, it is not possible to call non-Hack code from this mode. In addition, it is no longer permissible to directly construct arrays as they must have a type. The recommended way around this is to use a collection instead.

The default mode for Hack is `partial` and it is quite a bit more relaxed. You can call non-Hack code and leave methods untyped. Essentially you can write plain PHP in this mode.

A third level can be found in `decl` which I would not recommend using from a Hack project unless it cannot be avoided. It is a weird mishmash the Hack manual identifies could cause bugs—if no other mode is working for you though, it might be worth a try.

These modes affect the behavior of the parser and how strictly the type signatures are adhered to. My suggestion is you always work in the strictest mode possible.

To test the type signatures and constraints declared in your code from the command line you can create a simple new Hack project simply by creating a new folder and placing an empty file called `.hhconfig` inside it. Now include your Hack files in this directory as you work on the project and when you are ready to test execute `hh_client` from the same location via a terminal.

Also note Hack will not allow top level code in files it is to type check with the only exception granted for `require` and `require_once` keywords. All other code which would normally live at the top level should be included in a function called `main()`. An example of this in action can be found in Listing 5.2 found later in this chapter.

The types themselves are reasonably similar to PHP except you can use them everywhere. If you remember with PHP 5, you are not able to hint scalar function arguments. In Hack you have the following types just like in PHP:

Type	Description
Boolean	`true` or `false`
integer	Whole numbers (including negative numbers)
float	floating point numbers (decimals)
double	Alias of `float`
string	Textual information
array	Ordered map or key/value list
object	Instance of a class
resource	a reference to an external resource such as a file handle
NULL	represents a variable with no value
callable	As of PHP 5.4 a variable to can be treated as a function

On top of these basic types, Hack defines collection types that facilitate data collections and lists in a less generic way than PHP's all-purpose array. These include:

Collection	Description
Vector	an ordered list collection
ImmVector	as `Vector`, but immutable (unchangeable after initial assignment)
Map	an ordered dictionary style collection
ImmMap	as `Map`, but immutable
Set	list collection that stores unique values
ImmSet	as `Set`, but immutable
Pair	indexed collection that holds two values

These types handle common ways in which we have to deal with lists, but they take the weight off us to implement them as you would in PHP. To create a new collection you would define something like:

```
$vector = Vector {1, 2};
$vector->add(3);
// Vector(1, 2, 3)
```

For compatibility, you can still use arrays just as you would in PHP, but you can also make it more specific. The type of an array can be defined in terms of both its value and its key/index.

The key and value are simply defined:

```
array<int, string>
```

Where the array has an integer key and the value is a string, if you just want to specify the type of the value and not the key use:

```
array<string>
```

This allows the array to be type checked by the parser and stops the list from becoming a grab bag of values. When you operate on a list you want to be able to treat all the values in the same way with as little difficulty as possible. By specifying the type signature like this you can be assured that you will always get a string (or the type you specify).

```
class HackArray {
    public array<int, string> $array = [
        1 => 'ibizo',
        2 => 'umuntu',
        3 => 'inja',
    ];
}
```

Should you desire to have an immutable array then Hack makes this possible through the use of a tuple that can be defined as:

```
$t = tuple(1, 2, 3);
$sum = array_sum($t); // 6
```

As an immutable type once the tuple is defined it cannot be changed and it would result in an error to do so.

These arrays serve as a simple collection or the basics of more custom application targeted collection classes. If you need a collection such as Set then it is better to use the Set collection Hack provides than write your own. This is for two reasons, both primarily being efficiency; it is an easily recognizable structure to any Hack programmer and as it is part of the language it is optimized by default.

In addition to collections and arrays, Hack also defines other useful types such as Enum, Generic, Shape. In the case of Enum you can define an enumeration type which allows only a value specified with in the definition to be assigned to any variable. This is demonstrated as a blog post publication state in Listing 5.1.

Listing 5.1
```
01. enum BlogPostState: int {
02.     Published = 1;
03.     Queued = 0;
04.     Draft = -1;
05. }
06.
07. class BlogPost {
08.     public BlogPostState $state = BlogPostState::Published;
09.     public function getState(): BlogPostState {
10.         return $this->state;
11.     }
12. }
```

There are numerous uses for Enum type and it gives you a very simple storage mechanism for when Booleans are simply not enough.

Slightly less exciting is the addition of a *nullable* type hint for function parameters in the form of prepending them with a question mark (?). This allows you to indicate what parameters can accept a null value when defining a function. Generally, it would not feature heavily in functional code as it allows a null to be passed in where the application would be expecting solid type.

```
function spit(?string $rhyme) {
    return (string) $rhyme;
}
```

You could now call the `spit()` function with a parameter of `null` instead of the specified `string` and it would parse this without complaint.

```
$r1 = spit('Ibizo');
$r2 = spit(null);
```

Type Aliasing

Hack allows developers to alias internal types to new more specific names which can be used for more accurate type checking when dealing with function parameters and annotations. Sometimes this can be very useful, especially when dealing with strings. What are strings? Well they could be a date, a URL, an ISBN, a phone number or some other structured string it would be helpful to type, so they can be handled slightly differently.

```
type PhoneNumber = string;
```

Once the type is aliased it can then be used in normal type hinting situations like function arguments and return types.

```
$phoneNumber = '+44.790 000 0000';
function removePhoneNumberFormatting(PhoneNumber $pn) {
    return str_replace(
        ['+', '.', ' '],
        ['00', '', ''],
        $pn
    );
}
$dialable = removePhoneNumberFormatting($phoneNumber);
```

This is what Hack calls a type alias, but it also supports opaque type aliasing which is a more guarded version of the aliasing we have already seen. It hides the underlying type meaning which in strict mode it would not be able to be manipulated as a `string` in the case of the phone number above.

```
newtype PostDate = string;
```

One small caveat is in the file that `newtype` is declared you can use the type/value as if it were the underlying type. In the case of a string you could concatenate it in the originating file, but in any other file also using the type you would not be able to. If you have a file called `types.php` declaring an alias using the `newtype` keyword and subsequently a `blog_post.php` file using the type as in the example below, you would not be able to manipulate the URL slug from within `blog_post.php` as if it were string.

```
// in ·types.php·
newtype UrlSlug = string;

// in ·blog_post.php·
function fullUrl(UrlSlug $slug): UrlSlug {
    return SITE_URL . $slug;
}
$full_url = fullUrl('/2015-10-11/blog-post');
// It is incompatible with an object of type UrlSlug
```

I have yet to find a use for the `newtype` keyword as I have always wanted access to the underlying implementation and it seems to be akin to using `private` methods when writing code in a library class. It makes the code more difficult to use and adds little to no benefit in most situations. That is until you combine it with the `as` keyword; now you have what a plain `newtype` always should have been! A new type which cannot be type checked to its underlying type, but can be used with the underlying types operators. In the case of a new type based upon an integer this would mean you would then have access to the arithmetic operators such as `+`, `*`, `/` and `-` amongst others. Unlike `newtype` you now actually have a usable type!

Listing 5.2
```
01. // in ·types.php·
02. newtype PostId as int = int;
03.
04. function getPostId(int $id): PostId {
05.     return $id;
06. }
07.
08. // in ·blog_post.php·
09. function validateId(PostId $id): bool {
10.     return ($id > 1);
11. }
12.
13. function main(): void {
14.     $id = getPostId(10);
15.     validateId($id); // true
16. }
```

There are a few items of note in Listing 5.2 beginning with the use of a function (`getPostId()`) to obtain a value of type `PostId` from an `int`. The function accepts an `int`, but its return type is specified as `PostId` and this is enough to convince Hack any integer value passed through it is now a `PostId` when the value is returned.

In the `validateId()` function a comparison operator is used to check that the `PostId` is greater than one. This comparison operator would not work without the `as` keyword section in the original `newtype` definition.

This is also the first time we have seen the `main()` function in use within Hack. This is the default function the type checker bootstrap process will call when the project is built. Any top level code should go into this function or the Hack type checker will throw an error stating only `require` requests are allowable at the top level. Note a new type of `void` has been specified as the return type of this function as well. This means no value will be returned by the function in question.

Now let's break something! The type checker will get upset if you try to treat a Boolean return value as a `PostId` as shown below. It will not allow you to effectively convert a Boolean value to a `PostId` (an `int` underneath).

```
function checkInt(int $id): PostId {
    return is_int($id);
}
// Invalid argument, This is an object of type PostId, It is
// incompatible with a bool
```

Now we have a type which is usable with operators, but cannot be treated as its underlying type when type checking. This prevents an `integer` value from incorrectly being evaluated as a `PostId`.

Generics

Hack also allows the definition of generics which allow you to approach your work in a way previously impossible with PHP. You can define a data agnostic handling class which will be typed via inference at the point it is used—much like the Vector we reviewed earlier.

Generics provide a useful method of bringing some kind of type handling to PHPs sister language Hack. They perform this action by accepting any type such as a scalar (int, string, etc), arrays, and classes. Once the type has been set on an instance of a Generic it is only possible to add content of the same specified type to the Generic. So if a generic is created and assigned a value of type string then it will infer the whole generic is of type string and disallow the addition of values of other types.

All well and good, but this would not be a whole dose of help just on its own. So you can also add methods to the class definition to handle operations on its contents. This might include operations such as map() that assists with method execution against a list of values. Generics also allow you to write functions which can operate in a general way on data structures. This means you can write code to be used across types and prevent repeating formalisms for each different type.

You could achieve a similar effect with a set of PHP objects, instanceof checks and casts of the values. However, having language support for this feature allows you to concentrate on the business problem rather than attempting to implement your own type system.

Listing 5.3

```
01. class IO<T> {
02.     private T $data;
03.
04.     public function __construct(T $value) {
05.         $this->data = $value;
06.     }
07.
08.     public function toScreen() {
09.         echo (string) $this->data;
10.     }
11.
12.     public function write() {
13.         file_put_contents('/tmp/io_out', $this->data);
14.     }
15. }
```

In Listing 5.3 the type T is used to indicate the type that will be inferred when a variable is passed into it. You could think of it almost like a variable type—one not specified at the point of definition, but when first called. If you pass in a string the parser will set T to be a type of string otherwise when passing an array T will become a type of array.

A Generic can contain any value, but once a type (T) is chosen it puts tools in place to help you ensure only the type initially supplied is permissible for addition.

```
$a = new IO('Sawubona');
$a->toScreen(); // Sawubona
$b = new IO(10);
$b->write(); // '10' written to file
```

Looking at the code above, the variable $a will be an instance of IO with a T of string and $b would have a T of int. This inference of type to T is what makes a Generic a generic.

Another useful implementation can be to create a more universal list handling class which can be used to perform common operations on lists no matter the type they contain.

Listing 5.4
```
01. class MappableList<T> {
02.     public array<int, T> $data = [];
03.
04.     public function __construct(
05.         ?array<int, T> $initial_value = null
06.     ) {
07.         if($initial_value) {
08.             $this->data = $initial_value;
09.         }
10.     }
11.
12.     public function add(T $value) {
13.         $this->data[] = $value;
14.     }
15.
16.     public function map(callable $function) {
17.         return new MappableList(
18.             array_map($function, $this->data)
19.             );
20.     }
21. }
```

Listing 5.4 is deliberately more complicated and makes use of more Hack type checking with the array key and value types specified. In this case the type of the array value will adopt the type of T when the first value is assigned to the Generic. So if a value of type string is assigned, then both T and the array value with be set to type string.

MappableList also has a constructor with not only the array type specified on its parameter, but also the nullable ? prepended too. This allows the constructor to be called with the default value of null or by passing an array of the correct type as the initial value for the $data class property.

This facilitates the wrapped return value of the map() method so any time map is called it will return the result of the function mapping in a neatly wrapped up instance of MappableList.

Listing 5.5
```
01. $c = new MappableList;
02. $c->add('Sawubona');
03. $c->add('Ibizo');
04. $c->add('Inja');
05.
06. $xs = $c->map(function($item) {
07.     return strtoupper($item);
08. });
09.
10. // MappableList (
11. //     'SAWUBONA',
12. //     'IBIZO',
13. //     'INJA',
14. // )
```

Implementing a `Generic` will set the type of `T` and Listing 5.4 we have been very careful to specify `T` as the required type across the board. When we then call it in Listing 5.5 we must ensure we abide by the initial type set (`string` in this case) and all subsequent values must be of the same type.

The mapping called from Listing 5.5 is a simple anonymous function to convert all values in the list to uppercase. The `MappableList` class will then wrap this simple `array` list into an instance of itself returning a new `MappableList` with all the values in uppercase.

Shapes

Shapes allow a structured data type in Hack where records can be described and their "shape" later relied upon. This could be things like the product of a query, map coordinates, or other forms of structured data.

To declare a `Shape` you must include a type definition and layout how the contents of the structure will be set out.

```
type BlogPostShape = shape(
    'id' => int,
    'date' => string,
    'tags' => array<int, string>,
    'title' => string,
    'content' => string,
);
```

This structure can then be populated with data as evidence in Listing 5.6 with the blog post structure being filled out with some information relating to a fictional blog post.

Listing 5.6

```
01. $bp = shape(
02.     'id' => 10,
03.     'date' => '2015-05-08',
04.     'tags' => [
05.         'functional',
06.         'programming',
07.         'book',
08.     ],
09.     'title' => 'Blog post title',
10.     'content' => 'The content of the blog post goes here.',
11. );
12. print $bp['id']; // 10
```

Shapes provide a neat way of categorizing content based on the fields which are fulfilled and supplied. The structures can be type checked and then handled differently dependent upon the data and structure contained within them.

```
function blogPostToHtml(BlogPostShape $shape) {
    return "<h1>{$shape['title']}</h1>" . PHP_EOL
        . "<p>{$shape['content']}</p>";
}
$html_post = blogPostToHtml($bp);
// <h1>Blog post title</h1>
// <p>The content of the blog post goes here.</p>
```

Shapes are a simple and useful way to represent, store, and interrogate structured data in your Hack applications.

Lambda Expressions

Anonymous functions get a new sweeter syntax in Hack with the introduction of lambda expressions. Similar to PHP's closure a lambda expression can take in context from its surrounding environment. In fact, Hack does this implicitly to reduce the number of key strokes required. This effectively does away with the use keyword found in PHP and replaces it by automatically pulling in the environment variables. The only exception is input by reference, which must still be specified in a use clause and preceded by an ampersand.

That is one way to cut down on bloat, but Hack has another trick up its sleeve with the ==> shortcut for defining a lambda function. This is the essence of a Hack lambda expression.

An example of this is best described side-by-side with the equivalent PHP code. Not only does this make the syntax clearer, but it also very clearly shows the advantages of syntactic sugar. First, though, we need to define a simple helper function to execute a function with one supplied parameter.

```
function applyFunc($var, callable $func) {
    return $func($var);
}
```

In PHP we would then call it and in this case we are passing an anonymous function into it.

```
$add_one = function($v) {
    return $v + 1;
};

$x = applyFunc(1, $add_one); // 2
```

In Hack this could be written in a simpler and shorter manner reusing the apply() function from before.

```
$add_one = $v ==> $v + 1;
$y = applyFunc(1, $add_one);
```

Closures are even more compact with their implicit context.

```
$a = 'sawubona';
$ret = () ==> { return $a; }; // sawubona
```

As you can see in the example, because$func is in the same scope as $a the variable is automatically available inside the closure ($func). In PHP it would look a little longer:

```
$a = 'sawubona';
$func = function() use ($a) {
    return $a;
};
$func(); // sawubona
```

The last Hack example also demonstrates another trait of lambda expressions where if you do not have an argument you must use parenthesis at the beginning of your expression. This is also the case with expressions accepting multiple parameters.

```
$func = ($a, $b, $c) ==> { return $a . $b . $c; };
$z = $func('s', 'u', 'n'); // sun
```

PHP's lambdas and closures are very useful, but much like the rest of the language the syntax is very verbose. Hack brings a nice succinct syntax that still looks a lot like PHP. Dispensing with the need for a use clause is another simple way that the syntax is decluttered. The code becomes both easier to write and then later to read during maintenance. Smaller character counts are generally good when it comes to maintenance as it is less to read and therefore to have to build up in your mind. This map of execution we create in our minds is a high cognitive load these expressions help to reduce.

Much like other features of Hack adopted by PHP it would be great to see an RFC for the inclusion of lambda expressions with their implicit scope. Given the language changing nature though it would, unfortunately, seem unlikely it would make it past the voting phase.

Special (Magical) Attributes

There is no PHP equivalent of these special keywords in Hack bringing specialist functionality to classes. They add custom magic to classes in a similar way to PHP's `__toString()` or `__construct()` methods, but as annotations.

You can easily cache function results with the special `<<__Memoize>>` attribute which can be added to both functions and class methods. In the code that follows, you can see two calls to a function which returns a unique string yield the same result when the memoize attribute is added directly above the function definition—normally `$a` and `$b` would be different.

```
<<__Memoize>>
function getUniqueString(): string {
    return uniqid();
}
$a = getUniqueString();
$b = getUniqueString();
$c = ($a === $b); // true
```

This is a very simple annotation to add above any method or function to immediately give it memoized properties without having to complete any of the implementation yourself. There are a few things to note though about the parameters you can send to a function or method with this annotation. Only the following types may be passed in as arguments: `null`, `bool`, `int`, `float`, `string`, an implementation of `IMemoizeParam` and arrays containing any of the aforementioned types. In addition to this, parameters may not be passed by reference and should be defined within the parentheses of the function rather than varargs.

Less interesting are the `<<__Override>>` and `<<__ConsistentConstruct>>` attributes relating to class definitions within Hack. The first is implemented immediately before any class method and its purpose is to ensure consistency between your class and its parent. An error is triggered if the parent class does not contain a concrete implementation of the same method. This has the effect of letting you know a child class overrides a particular method when you attempt to refactor it out of the parent class.

If `<<__ConsistentConstruct>>` is added above a class definition then it has the effect of telling the Hack parser to check all classes that extend it use a compatible `__construct()` method definition. Sometimes this may not be useful and you might like to prevent it from applying to a subclass you are writing by adding `<<UNSAFE_Construct>>` above the `__construct()` method. Hack will then ignore it and rely on the fact the programmer who wrote it has accounted for consistency instead!

If you want to use these special attributes together you can separate them with commas to form a list between the angle brackets as demonstrated below:

```
class SpecialAttributesExample {
    <<__Override, __Memoize>>
    function getUniqueString(): string {
        return uniqid();
    }
}
```

Conclusion

Hack provides a number of nice extras and some improved syntax over PHP—this is more of an incentive to use HHVM than faster running PHP scripts. Most of what I have covered in this chapter are features that set Hack apart. For the most part, it implements PHP. This means that although not documented here, you still get functionality for a variable number of arguments, the SPL, and other PHP language functions. These are simply implemented in the same manner and syntax as PHP.

Of course, I have also glossed over a few other features of Hack you may find useful in object-oriented code or where it has felt like too much of a detour to include here. These features are all very well documented in the Hack manual and also in various Facebook blog posts should you wish to delve deeper into the language.

Chapter

6

Patterns

"Monads are return types that guide you through the happy path."

–Erik Meijer (Computer Scientist, *@headinthebox*)

In functional programming there are repeating patterns just as in any other programming style. This is in fact a major source of interest in functional programming from unacquainted coders, as it brings with it concise code.

Software patterns are generally agreed best practices for completing similar tasks in a universally identifiable and understood way. Much like object oriented programming, functional code also has a number of patterns you will regularly see. These patterns assist in making more composable functions allowing for greater reuse across various problem domains. Not only this, but they can help to make your API more consistent for those implementing any functional library you might have written. If the pattern is followed then implementers can accurately anticipate the result when they call the pattern from their code.

Patterns can be reproduced across a large number of types easily and quickly in most functional languages, but in PHP we need to lay the ground work ourselves first. Looking to the world of mathematics there are far more patterns than we will cover here. Some patterns are borrowed from the ideas implemented in the Haskell programming language, which can be a little difficult to reproduce given PHPs weak type system. It is, however, possible and they help to present excellent ways of producing reusable code.

It does not mean we will avoid implementing difficult patterns though with applicatives and monads both discussed. Some might suggest only a Haskell programmer should be interested in these formalisms, but they would be short sighted. It is easier to learn a pattern in a language you already know well than a completely foreign one. And, the patterns are actually useful in PHP code too, as we will explore further into the book.

Reusable patterns are great and what we all strive for as programmers. Good, functional code takes this up a notch and tries to abstract all operations into reusable and immutable code. To this end we will now explore some common and some complex patterns in functional PHP code.

Should you be unwilling to push the boundaries of PHP, turn back now and wallow in your safe billabong (oxbow lake, resaca, bayou). The next section has a raft and it is headed for the white water!

Head and Tail

We will start with a very simple pattern first though to ease our way into it. When working with lists and recursion it can be very helpful to be able to easily obtain the first element of an array (the head) and what is known as the tail of the array. Head, given an array, will return the first value from that array.

```
function head(array $arr) {
    return reset($arr);
}
head([1, 2, 3, 4, 5]); // 1
```

At the other end of the equation we have tail that will return a list with all but the first value in the array contained in it.

```
function tail(array $arr) {
    return array_slice($arr, 1);
}
tail([1, 2, 3, 4, 5]); // [2, 3, 4, 5]
```

These two functions can be used together to work through a list using recursion.

```
function print_items(array $arr) {
    echo head($arr) . '-';
    if(tail($arr)) print_items(tail($arr));
}
print_items([1, 2, 3, 4, 5]); // 1-2-3-4-5-
```

Flattening lists

Lists of lists can be very helpful when dealing with complex datasets or when transforming an array via `array_map()` where it would return an array from the applied function. In some instances though, you have a list of lists that really should just be one list with all values at the top level. The problem could look something like:

```
$arr = [1, 2, 3, 4, 5];
$divisor = 10.5;
$arr2 = array_map(function($x) use ($divisor) {
    return [$x, $x / $divisor, $x % $divisor];
}, $arr);
```

Continued Next Page

```
// [
//    [1, 0.095238095238095233, 1],
//    [2, 0.19047619047619047, 2],
//    [3, 0.2857142857142857, 3],
//    [4, 0.38095238095238093, 4],
//    [5, 0.47619047619047616, 5]
// ]
```

Now you need to `array_sum()` all the values, but you have a multi-dimensional array. You want to flatten your list.

```
$arr3 = flatten($arr2);
// [
//    1, 0.095238095238095233, 1, 2, 0.19047619047619047, 2,
//    3, 0.2857142857142857, 3, 4, 0.38095238095238093, 4,
//    5, 0.47619047619047616, 5
// ]
```

After flattening the array all values are at the top level of the array and it is no longer multi-dimensional so we are now able to perform that all important `array_sum()` call.

```
array_sum($arr3); // 31.428571428571
```

PHP does not come with a `flatten()` function by default—as you might have suspected—and we are going to have to write one ourselves as in Listing 6.1. To make it more flexible we will add a maximum depth argument so an implementer can decide how many levels of their array they want to be flattened—starting from the top most dimension. Additionally it is often very useful for associative array keys to be maintained after the transformation so index access is not affected.

Listing 6.1

```
01. function flatten(array $array, $max_depth = null, $curr_depth = 1) {
02.     $out = [];
03.     foreach($array as $key => $val) {
04.         if(is_array($val)) {
05.             if(is_null($max_depth) || $curr_depth < $max_depth) {
06.                 $val = flatten($val, $max_depth, $curr_depth + 1);
07.             }
08.             $out = array_merge($out, $val);
09.         } elseif(is_int($key)) {
10.             $out[] = $val;
11.         } else {
12.             $out[$key] = $val;
13.         }
14.     }
15.     return $out;
16. }
```

This definition of `flatten()` will maintain associative keys and reset integer keys. It will flatten all dimensions of an array to one unless `$max_depth` specifies otherwise. It is common to only flatten an array by one level so a helpful function to have on hand is `flatten_one()`, which can be written in terms of `flatten()`.

```
function flatten_one(array $array) {
    return flatten($array, 1);
}
```

This is more obvious and easier to read when reviewing code than simply using `flatten($arr, 1)` all over the place in code (it is easier to search/`grep` for too).

Now that we have a working `flatten_one()` implementation, we can perform an `array_map()` with keys in a much easier way than before by making use of a closure to handle the requirement for keys.

```
function map_with_keys(array $array, callable $func) {
    $ks = array_keys($array);
    $fx = function($key) use ($array, $func) {
        return [$key => $func($key, $array[$key])];
    };
    return flatten_one(array_map($fx, $ks));
}
```

Instead of trying to work through the values of the array we can iterate over the keys above and then obtain the value later using the key inside `$fx`. To ensure that keys are maintained during the operation `$fx` returns an associative array that is later flattened using `flatten_one()`.

```
map_with_keys(
    ['a' => 1, 'b' => 2],
    function($k, $v) {
        return $v . $k;
    }
); // ['a' => '1a', 'b' => '2b']
```

With the keys being passed to our callback function it is now possible to incorporate the key into reduce operations and make use of it.

```
reduce_with_keys(
    ['a' => 1, 'b' => 2],
    function($acc, $k, $v) {
        return $acc . $k . $v;
    },
    ''
); // a1b2
```

As you can see in the highly contrived example above, the array is reduced through string concatenation. The resultant string contains both the keys and the values of each element within the array.

Handling Your NULLS

There are a number of functions in PHP—and I am sure many more in the legacy userland code you work on—returning NULL when no record can be found, for example. When you then call the function, you cannot be sure if it will return a record as you expect or a null value, which violates the principle a function should always return the same type so it can be handled in the same way.

We have previously implemented PHP's `array_reduce()` function, and it serves again as a great example. When it is fed an empty array, it will return NULL. Imagine the result of our reduce operation were to be passed into a function expecting to receive an integer, then it would trigger an error from PHP's parser. There are a few ways to handle these null values and protect your code from unforeseen errors.

In the case of `array_reduce()`, you can simply set an initial value as the third parameter to the function. This initial value will be returned if the input array is empty. Otherwise, it will be used as the base value to add each reduce operation to.

If you do not have control over the code you are calling or you are implementing a function that doesn't allow for a default return value, then you can make use of the following two techniques.

The first is a very simple solution using the implicit return value property of PHP's ternary operator. This works by leaving the second expression in the ternary operation empty like so:

```
$var = get_record() ?: array();
```

This code will assign the return value of `get_record()` to `$var` unless it is null in which case it will assign the empty array specified as the third expression of the ternary in the example.

A new arrival in PHP 7 is the `null` coalescence infix operator. Unlike the short ternary we examined earlier it will perform the `isset` operation for you. Effectively, the new syntax offers an easy way of saying "if isset and not empty return the value of this variable". This is known as an issetor operation where the value is returned if it is set or it calls the next operator.

```
$a = null;
$b = 10;
$c = $a ?? $b; // int(10)
```

It is also possible to chain the operation with many calls to get the first item returning a non-`null` value.

```
$v = null;
$w = null;
$x = null;
$y = 10;
$z = $v ?? $w ?? $x ?? $y; // int(10)
```

You can also do this with function calls instead of variables just as easily.

```
function get_result() {
    return null;
}
function get_another_result() {
    return null;
}
function get_default() {
    return 10;
}
$rt = get_result() ?? get_another_result() ?? get_default();
```

This is a handy short syntax for dealing with nulls in PHP 7. A good enough reason to upgrade to PHP 7 in its own right!

Now I must address a minor matter I glossed over for brevity's sake in the previous descriptions. It is not only a return value of NULL that will trigger a replacement. PHP also considers the following values to evaluate to false:

- false, of course
- an integer set to 0
- a float of 0.0
- an empty string or the string value "0"
- arrays containing no elements
- SimpleXML objects created from empty tags
- values of NULL

What if you only want to replace NULL values? Unfortunately, you are out of luck with the native PHP offerings, but Johannes Schmitt has written the php-option library[1]. His library ports functionality similar to Scala's Option values[2] to PHP.

Fortunately, it allows you to be more specific about when to supply a replacement value, such as in the next example which only replaces a value of NULL or an integer.

```
function get_safe_record() {
    $record = get_record();
    return (!is_null($record) && !is_int($record))
        ? new \PhpOption\Some($record)
        : \PhpOption\None::create();
}

$record = get_safe_record()
    ->getOrElse(array());
```

If you only want to protect code from null values, then you can use the fromValue() static method instead:

```
function get_safe_record() {
    return \PhpOption\Option::fromValue(get_record());
}
```

There is another advantage of this library; you can chain calls to orElse() so the code may try multiple alternatives to resolve the null return value.

```
$record = get_cached_record()
    ->orElse(get_api_record())
    ->orElse(create_new_record());
```

The code above simulates talking to a set of records available via a third-party API. If it can't find a cached record, then it will attempt to pull it across from the API. Were that to also fail, then it will create a new record and return it instead. As you can see, these techniques can be employed to assist us in our goal of avoiding flow control and assignment statements like those in the imperative provided in Listing 6.2 for comparison.

Listing 6.2

```
01. function get_safe_record() {
02.     $record = get_cached_record();
03.
04.     if(is_null($record)) {
05.         $record = get_api_record();
06.     }
07.
08.     if(is_null($record)) {
09.         $record = create_new_record();
10.     }
11.
12.     return $record;
13. }
```

[1] php-option: https://github.com/schmittjoh/php-option
[2] Scala Option values: http://www.scala-lang.org/api/current/index.html#scala.Option

Furthermore, if the code you are talking to requires you to instantiate objects, then you can employ lazy loading via php-option's `getOrCall()` method to stop PHP from creating the instance until it is actually required.

```
$record = get_safe_record()->getOrCall(function() {
   return ORM::for_table('records');
});
```

Dealing with null values in PHP can be tricky, but with the help of these patterns, you can mitigate the errors which would otherwise interrupt your code or require flow control statements and defensive programming.

Composition

It can often be helpful to combine functions to create reusable and more complex functions. The return value of each function is passed into the next, and the result of the last function is the final value returned. In mathematics and computer science, this process is known as composition.

PHP does not currently understand function composition, so we must define a new function to implement the logic:

```
function compose($a, $b) {
   return function() use ($a, $b) {
      $args = func_get_args();
      return $b(call_user_func_array($a, $args));
   };
}
```

This function accepts two functions as parameters, which are then composed together by `$b()` being passed the result of function `$a()`. The `compose()` function also handles applying the supplied arguments to `$a()`. It's important the return value/type from `$a()` is expected as an input parameter to `$b()`, or you will trigger a PHP error. Should you need to pass multiple arguments from `$a()` to `$b()`, then you will need to return an array as the result of `$a()`.

Now, let's put this composer into action:

```
$a = function($val) {
   return str_word_count($val);
};
$b = function($val) {
   return $val - 2;
};
$c = compose($a, $b);
$c('Here is some text to word count.'); // 5
```

In this contrived example, you can see two functions being composed with the first obtaining a simple word count from a supplied string and the second subtracting two from any integer passed into it. When the two functions are composed, the resulting function is `$c()`, which takes one string parameter and returns an integer value.

Partial Functions

Partial Function Application

Sometimes when you are operating on a list of values, it can be helpful to apply a function to it without knowing all the parameter values at the point of definition. For example, imagine a function which gets the first character of each item in the list as shown:

```php
$first_char = function($string) {
    return substr($string, 0, 1);
};
$mapped = array_map($first_char, ['foo', 'bar', 'baz']);
// array('f', 'b', 'b')
```

First, we create a new anonymous function, `$first_char`, which calls `substr()` and sets two of that function's parameters to the defaults of `0` and `1`. This partial function is then applied to a list of words by PHP's `array_map()`. While this solves a problem, it is not the most elegant of code and basically boils down to function wrapping. There is a PHP library called React/Partial[3] which makes this process easier and adds syntactic sugar to the exercise.

To make this clearer, here is an example of the React/Partial function in use from their documentation.

```php
use React\Partial;

$first_char = Partial\bind('substr', Partial\...(), 0, 1);
$mapped = array_map($first_char, [foo', 'bar', 'baz']);
// array('f', 'b', 'b')
```

`Partial\...()` is a placeholder which will be replaced by the value passed in at run time, which in this example is each item in the list `['foo', 'bar', 'baz']`.

At the time of writing, there is also a PHP RFC for adding partial function application to the core of PHP using a new `curry` keyword[4] and the same UTF-8 ellipsis as React/Partial for the placeholder. Before going further though, I must address the name—curry—as it is not actually currying, but partial function application.

The two terms refer to two distinct processes for reducing the number of parameters a function accepts, but they are often conflated. It cannot be denied the term curry is snappier than partial function application despite the potential for confusion. For now, we will gloss over it, but in the next section you will see some true currying.

> To learn more about PHP's RFC process, I would recommend a quick look through Christopher Jones's blog post[5].

---

[3]   React/Partial: https://github.com/reactphp/partial
[4]   Currying RFC: https://wiki.php.net/rfc/currying
[5]   The Mysterious PHP RFC Process and How You Can Change the Web:
      http://phpa.me/oracle-jones-php-rfc

Currying

So what is it really? Currying relies on the principle that it is possible to treat almost any function as a partial function of just one argument. To facilitate the currying process, the return values of the functions are actually functions themselves. Each parameter passed to the original function will become a function that is returned.

With closure support now available in PHP, it is possible to emulate currying. Let's step through a manually curried example to give you an idea of what's happening internally.

```php
$x = function($start) {
   return function($length) use ($start) {
      return function($string) use ($start, $length) {
         return substr($string, $start, $length);
      };
   };
};
```

As you can see, this is very similar to the code example from the partial function application examples earlier. Believe it or not, when this code is run, it will achieve the same result. In a more formula-orientated sense, our function has gone from ((a, b, c) -> d) to (a -> b -> c -> d).

What is the advantage of this over a partial function application? You can form many partial functions at run time and at any stage in the function chain. Partial function applications on the other hand define the functions "partialness" at declaration.

With that out of the way, we can get on with using a manual curry operation in the following example:

```php
$a = $x(0);
$b = $a(1);
$b('foo'); // 'f'
```

First, we pass in the character offset we want `substr()` to use by feeding 0 to `$x()`. Next up, we set the length of the string to return by calling `$a(1)`. You will probably have noted `$a()` is the return value from the previous line of code. Finally, we can pass in a string for the code to operate on for the return value of the last line of code (`$b()`).

We can infer from this `$b()` is the same as `$first_char()` in our partial function application example. If we want to get the first character from another string, then we could just call `$b()`:

```php
$b('bar'); // 'b'
$b('wena'); // 'w'
```

However, if we later wanted to get the first two characters, then we could run the following code:

```php
$c = $a(2);
$c('foo'); // 'fo'
$c('bar'); // 'ba'
$c('wena'); // 'we'
```

Here we are generating a new function (`$c()`) by setting the length to 2 so our new partial function returns the first two letters of the supplied string. Once again, as you can see, it is using the return value of `$x(0)` (a function) to pass in the length required. All well and good you might say, but awfully verbose. The basic mechanics in the code samples have been automated in Listing 6.3 using the curry functionality in the nicmart/Functionals library.

Listing 6.3

```
01. use Functionals\Functionals;
02. $x = Functionals::curry(function($start, $length, $string) {
03.    return substr($string, $start, $length);
04. });
05.
06. $a = $x(0);
07. $b = $a(1);
08. $b('foo'); // 'f'
09.
10. $c = $a(2);
11. $c('foo'); // 'fo'
```

Elfet/Functional also has the concept of currying, but I prefer the implementation in nicmart/Functionals. The details of the libraries mentioned here are covered in more depth further on.

There is no technical reason or special meaning to be gleaned from the name of this functional methodology, but you are probably wondering where the term currying does come from. Well, it has nothing to do with the delicious food of the same name—although every time you curry a function, you may experience pangs of hunger. Just me? I doubt it!

The technique is in fact named after a mathematician, Haskell Curry, who incidentally gives his name to the Haskell programming language, among others. There is some controversy around the naming as it is widely understood Moses Schönfinkel laid the ground work for the combinatory logic, and therefore, currying should perhaps be known as Schönfinkelization.

Whatever you choose to call it, it's a very powerful technique as demonstrated by Haskell (the programming language, not the man) making use of currying for all functions which accept more than one parameter.

Pipelines

Pipelines make code chaining clearer and simpler by bringing some lightweight structure to the exercise. While this is a very simple technique and it is not strictly a functional pattern it is useful. Anywhere you want to chain three or more functions it starts to pay dividends.

A common example can be found in formatting strings where PHP's API requires a number of function calls to transform text. Say you want to accept a string and ensure only the first letter is capitalized and then truncate it to six characters. To achieve this in PHP you would chain `strtolower()`, `ucfirst()` and `substr()`. This is simple enough with code like this:

```
$a = 'Woza My Fohloza';
$b = ucfirst(strtolower(substr($a, 0, 6)));
// $b = 'Woza M';
```

What if you now want to replace all spaces with hyphens? Simple—just add a call to `str_replace()` in the chain and mess abounds!

A simpler way of doing it is to use a pipeline of functions to which you supply the list of functions you wish to run as an array.

First though, we need to change the functions we saw earlier that do not accept our string as their first argument. We do not need to worry about `substr($str, 0, 6)` as it does accept the string as its first argument (`$str`).

Unfortunately `str_replace(' ', '-', $str)` does not though so it must be partially applied to create a function that accepts one argument. You could also simply wrap the function with another to achieve the same result, but we will use the React/Partial library in the examples here. In the following example we put `str_replace(' ', '-', $str)` into a partial function with just one argument so it can be chained in a pipeline.

```
$space_replace = Partial\bind('str_replace', ' ', '-', Partial\ ());
```

Now we have a set of correctly ordered argument functions that can be applied to the supplied data. The next step is to produce a pipeline function which will iterate over the list of functions applying them to the supplied piece of data each time.

This can be defined in terms of reduce in PHP with as shown below illustrating a straight forward array reduce which applies each function against the carried value as we saw in the `array_map()` section. One nifty feature of this pipeline implementation is support for subsequent parameters to be sent through with a function specification by supplying an array.

Listing 6.4

```
01. function pipeline() {
02.     $argument = head(func_get_args());
03.     $funcs = tail(func_get_args());
04.     return array_reduce($funcs, function($carry, $f) {
05.         if (is_array($f)) {
06.             return call_user_func_array(
07.                 head($f),
08.                 array_merge([$carry], tail($f))
09.             );
10.         }
11.         return $f($carry);
12.     }, $argument);
```

A typical usage of this function might look something like the following, where a series of string manipulation functions are called in sequence against a string value.

```
$c = pipeline(
    $a,
    ['substr', 0, 6],
    $space_replace,
    'strtolower',
    'ucfirst',
);
```

You will note that the `substr()` reference is sent through as an array—this allows you to pass through subsequent parameters to a function. The first argument to `substr()` will always be the first argument supplied to the `pipeline()` call and the additional parameters specified in the array will make up parameters two and three for `substr()`. This effectively means that in our previous example `substr()` will be called as `substr($a, 0, 6)`. It is similar in implementation to a similar function in Elixir (|>/2)[6].

[6] Elixir (|>/2): http://elixir-lang.org/docs/stable/elixir/Kernel.html

With this very simple example out of the way we can move onto a more useful pipeline that can operate on a list of values below. It first maps over the list of data and then passes it into pipeline() defined earlier.

```
function pipeline_list($functions, $list_data) {
  return array_map(function($data) use ($functions) {
    return call_user_func_array(
        'pipeline',
        array_merge([$data], $functions)
    );
  }, $list_data);
}
```

When given a list of string values the pipeline_list() function can iterate over them and execute the list of functions in Listing 6.5.

Listing 6.5
```
01. $d = pipeline_list(
02.     [
03.         $first_six,
04.         $space_replace,
05.         'strtolower',
06.         'ucfirst',
07.     ],
08.     [
09.         'Woza My Fohloza',
10.         'Ndihamba Nawe',
11.         'Umqombothi',
12.         'Pata Pata'
13.     ]
14. );
15. // array (
16. //     'Woza-m',
17. //     'Ndiham',
18. //     'Umqomb',
19. //     'Pata-p',
20. // )
```

If you need a simple way of applying a series of functions to a value or a list of values then a pipeline could be a good way of keeping your code a little neater. It's easier to see a list of functions in the order they will be applied rather than reading a series of consecutive functions from the inside out as well.

Pattern Matching

A feature of many functional programming languages is the ability to pattern match input and produce different outcomes based upon that. In some ways it could be thought of as a more powerful switch statement in PHP. The parser will start with the top match and work its way down until it finds the first pattern that matches.

PHP does not ship with a feature like this by default so we will have to implement one ourselves, which is actually easier than it might seem. It will have some shortcomings and it certainly won't be as pretty or powerful as those you get to use in Scala or Haskell, but they are useful and that is why they are important to this book.

To make the process of understanding this easier, we will start with how a pattern will look and then move onto the actual implementation details later. The first thing that is important to a pattern is the value it will operate on. We will set this as the first function argument. In addition, we also need to specify the patterns this value should be tested against and—should it match—what the outcome or action should be.

Keeping the pattern syntax simple and clean is difficult in PHP, but array notation gives us a nice look with => that could be analogous to then. This gives the definition meaning; if matched => do this.

```
pattern(
    new stdClass(),
    [
        'is_string' => function($x) { return ucfirst($x); },
        'stdClass' => 'it is a stdClass',
        '_' => 'the default value'
    ]
); // it is a stdClass
```

The pattern in the example above is relatively simple—the value to operate on is an instance of stdClass(), which is passed in as the first argument to pattern. The second argument is the list of patterns to test it against.

As it works through the patterns, the parser will execute each test (the array keys) against the value (stdClass). Where the test returns true, the value of the matching element in the array will be returned or executed if it is a callable. Make sure that you put the more specific patterns first in the list of patterns passed to the function.

In this case it will run through the following assessment process under the covers:

1. is_string(stdClass)—evaluates to false as stdClass is an object
2. is_a(stdClass, 'stdClass')—evaluates to true and assessment is halted
3. returns the string it is a stdClass

Were it not to have matched against the first two then it would of moved onto the default _ pattern, which matches anything. This is the same character as used by both Scala and Haskell in their pattern matching syntax to indicate a default.

Now you have seen example and understand how it is supposed to work. We need to actually implement the pattern() function.

```
function pattern($data, array $patterns) {
    foreach($patterns as $test => $result) {
        if(pattern_exec_test($test, $data)) {
            return pattern_exec_result($result, $data);
        }
    }
}
```

As previously discussed, the pattern function accepts the value to operate against first and as its second argument it will accept and array of patterns. These should be given in a format where the array key is the pattern or test and the array value is the desired output or a callable that will return the desired output.

Working through the supplied pattern list in order the function will apply the pattern or test to the supplied value ($data) and where it matches it will return the specified result.

Given our requirements for pattern matching there are a few tests we will need to support in the `pattern_exec_test()` function and order is important here too. Where the given pattern is a string containing:

Pattern	Matches	Test performed
_	Any value	Any value is accepted so we just return true to short circuit the matching process. Use this to specify a default match.
stdClass, MyNamespace\ExampleClass, MyNamespace\ExampleInterface, etc.	Against a class or interface name	Checks $data is an object and if so whether it matches the specified class or interface (eg. ExampleInterface) using PHP's is_a() function.
is_string, is_bool, etc or an anonymous function or closure	Any callable	If the pattern is considered a callable by PHP then call it against the supplied value ($data). Note that $data is passed as the first and only argument to the callable so you will need to use partial function application to use functions that do not meet this requirement. As an example a pattern of is_string would become a function call of is_string($data).
a string	Compares as string	A simple === equality check between the supplied value ($data) and a string literal. For example 'a string' === $data.

To match these rules of assessment we will need a simple function like:

```
function pattern_exec_test($test, $data) {
    if('_' === $test) {
        return true;
    } else if(is_object($data) &&
        (interface_exists($test) || class_exists($test))) {
        return is_a($data, $test);
    } else if(is_callable($test)) {
        return $test($data);
    } else if($data === $test) {
        return true;
    }
    return false;
}
```

Hopefully, this is easy to understand and interpret using the table shown earlier.

Finally we get to the `pattern_exec_result()` function, which is called when a pattern is matched. This function will be given either a string or a callable as it's first parameter and the original specified value ($data) as its second argument. If it is a callable then it will apply the callable to $data and return the result. Otherwise it will simple return the result as it was supplied.

```
function pattern_exec_result($result, $data) {
    return is_callable($result) ?
        $result($data) :
        $result;
}
```

This provides simple pattern matching, but it is also inherently naive and there are a few rough edges given the input must be a string. As a simple example of one of these, imagine if you wanted to test against a string literal of is_string or _—you cannot because they are special values (a callable and a special value to pattern() respectively). Of course you can solve these issues in a few ways, but in the interests of keeping these examples simple and clearly communicating the principles, it is left to you, dear reader, to do so.

Even with these limitations, it is possible to write some shorter and potentially clearer code using this method. To help understand how this might be done, we will finish up with a couple of worked examples where pattern() is put to some use.

First, a string matcher that transforms the value by applying ucfirst() to the specified value (functional php).

```
pattern(
    'functional php',
    [
        'stdClass' => 'it is stdClass',
        'is_string' => function($x) { return ucfirst($x); },
        '_' => 'the default value'
    ]
); // Functional php
```

The following example demonstrates the default properties of the special _ string.

```
pattern(
    new DateTimeImmutable(),
    [
        'stdClass' => 'it is stdClass',
        'is_string' => function($x) { return ucfirst($x); },
        '_' => 'the default value'
    ]
); // the default value
```

Given that a DateTimeImmutable() will not match stdClass or an is_string() test then it will fall back to the default _.

You can use the pattern() function to test the type of a supplied value and then apply transformations to it or return a static value. This gives you a simple and clean interface for performing these kinds of operations with out polluting your code with if-else hell or switch statements.

Functors

We have already seen PHP's functors using the __invoke() method in a class, but as we also discovered, this is merely an object function and not a true functor. To understand what constitutes a functor, we must delve a little deeper into the theory. Simple values can have a function applied to them with little fuss:

```
function x($v) {
    return $v * 2;
}
echo x(2); // 4
```

It works as expected, but what if this value were stored in a context? To make it easier to picture this, imagine a context acts much like having a value wrapped up inside a box. This context will affect the result of any function called against the value it contains. Of course, our function x() does not expect anything but a simple numeric value, and if the value has been bound up into a context, it can no longer be directly applied in the same manner.

To facilitate this, you will need a universal way of calling functions against these bound values. In Haskell, this is the job of a function called fmap, but in PHP, you must write your own code to emulate the functionality.

Below is a very simple PHP functor that matches the code we saw earlier.

```php
class x
{
    public function __invoke($v) {
        return $v * 2;
    }
}


$x = new x;
echo $x(2); // 4
```

To add a context to the input value, we need to declare a simple type class, which will wrap up the value in a box (see Figure 6.1):

Figure 6.1: Wrapping the Value in Just

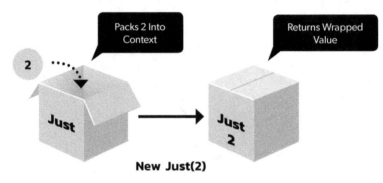

```php
class Just
{
    public $value = null;

    public function __construct($value) {
        $this->value = $value;
    }
}
```

If we now try to apply the PHP functor to this wrapped value, we will witness an almighty crunch resulting in a PHP notice:

```php
echo $x(new Just(2));
// PHP Notice: Object of class Just could not be converted
// to int
```

To fix this, we must create an emulation of Haskell's `fmap()` function in PHP (see Figure 6.2), which is actually quite simple:

```
function fmap($function, $just) {
    return $function($just->value);
}
echo fmap($x, new Just(2)); // 4
```

Figure 6.2: Applying a Function to a Just

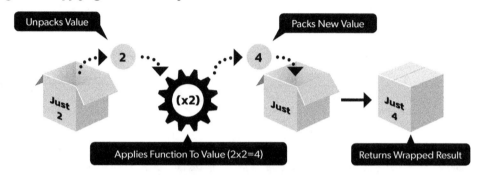

The beauty of `fmap()` is that it knows how to unpack the value from its context before applying a function to it.

So far so good. However, functors should also return a wrapped value back (Figure 6.2) so we need to modify `fmap()` slightly:

```
function fmap($function, $just) {
    return new Just($function($just->value));
}
$result = fmap($x, new Just(2)); // Just(4)
```

So far, the code we have seen is not exactly universal as I had promised—just try applying `fmap()` to a list of values! To make it easier for `fmap()`, we must define some more data types and specify how `fmap()` is to be applied to each one. To start with, we will create an interface our type classes will implement:

```
interface FunctorInterface
{
    /**
     * Defines how fmap should apply this data type
     * @param callable $function
     * @return FunctorInterface
     */
    public function __invoke($function);
}
```

Defining the interface makes it possible to type check using PHP's `instanceOf`, and to make it easier on yourself, define an abstract class (Listing 6.6) for the type classes to extend.

Listing 6.6
```
01. abstract class Functor implements FunctorInterface {
02.     protected $container = null;
03.
04.     public function __construct($data = null) {
05.         $this->set($data);
06.     }
07.
08.     public function get() {
09.         return $this->container;
10.     }
11.
12.     public function set($value) {
13.         $this->container = $value;
14.     }
15. }
```

> You may be wondering why I have defined both an abstract class and an interface. This is a personal preference for a couple of reasons, stemming from the fact I firmly believe only interfaces should be used to form contracts and type hints. This allows anyone to replace the abstract with one of their own and just implement the interface, so your code will still work. The second and most useful part of this is PHP can implement many interfaces, but it can only extend one class. By not forcing an implementer to extend your abstract, they may inherit from any class they desire.
>
> This is the reason interfaces exist to my mind and attempting to replace them with abstract classes instead could lead to hampered interoperability. Users of any library will thank you if you follow this pattern, even though it may feel like you are repeating yourself at the time.

As you can see, this is really quite a simple container class which stores a value in `$container`. Next up, we can improve upon the earlier `Just` type class with:

```
class Just extends Functor {
    public function __invoke($function) {
        return new Just($function($this->container));
    }
}
```

This is the first time we are using `__invoke()` to control how `fmap()` applies a function to the wrapped value. In the case of `Just`, it simply calls the supplied function against the wrapped value and returns a new instance of `Just` containing the result. To support this style, we must also make a few more changes to our `fmap()` function.

```
class NotAFunctorException extends \Exception {}

function fmap($function, $functor) {
    if(!($functor instanceOf FunctorInterface)) {
        throw new NotAFunctorException(
            'fmap must be passed a Functor'
        );
    }
    return $functor($function);
}
```

To stop illegal usage of this function, it will throw an exception if the value passed to it does not implement the `FunctorInterface` we created previously. It then simply calls the functor and passes in the function to be applied. This is where the `__invoke()` method in the `Just` type class steps in and performs the actual function application against the wrapped value and returns a new instance of `Just` containing the results.

Below is an example that puts our new `fmap()` and `Just` functionality to the test.

```
fmap($x, new Just(2)); // Just(4);
```

At this point, it makes sense to review the two laws governing what a functor must do and how it must appear to surrounding code. The first functor law ensures the `fmap()` function itself does not change the returned value, for only `$x()` in our example is allowed to work on the contained value. This can be written in a formulaic manner as `fmap id = id`, which will make more sense when addressed in the example code further on. You can think of `fmap()` as an impartial facilitator which, while it is incredibly important, should have no effect on the final output.

It is also stated in the second law, composing two functions—and subsequently mapping the resulting function over a functor—should be the same as first mapping one function over the function and then mapping the second one. This can be written as `fmap(f . g) = fmap f . fmap g`, and it is essentially a protection against `fmap()` altering the return value.

Let's test the `Just` functor against these laws to prove its status as a functor, starting with the first law in:

```
$id = function($value) {
    return $value;
};
fmap($id, new Just(2)); // Just(2);
$id(new Just(2)); // Just(2);
```

It is immediately clear we have achieved a pass against the first law. Next, the second law can also be proven for `Just`:

```
$a = function($value) {
    return $value + 1;
};
$b = function($value) {
    return $value + 2;
};
$c = compose($a, $b);
fmap($c, new Just(2)); // Just(5);

fmap($a, fmap($b, new Just(2))); // Just(5);
```

Once again, you can see the second law holds as well, and we can congratulate ourselves on having created our first functor. However, we have used more code to reach the same result—why would that ever be useful?

Next, we define the class Nothing, a friendly data type representation of an empty or null value to prove we can benefit from our new universal style.

```
class Nothing extends Functor {
    public function __invoke($function) {
        return new Nothing;
    }
}
```

I know it was a bit of a letdown, but wait, there's more! What if we want to work on those lists mentioned earlier?

```
class Collection extends Functor {
    public function __invoke($function) {
        return new Collection(
            array_map(function($value) use ($function) {
                return $function($value);
            }, $this->container)
        );
    }
}
```

Here, the Collection class represents a wrapped list or array, and the __invoke() defined within knows how to apply a function to each item in the list. Now you can see the power of abstracting out some of the functionality:

```
$list = new Collection([
    1,
    2,
    3,
]);
$resultList = fmap($x, $list); // Collection(2, 4, 6)
```

You will have noticed a useful function on the Functor abstract class called get(), and we can use it now to extract the actual value back out of the context.

```
$array = $resultList->get(); // array(2, 4, 6)
```

Functors are an excellent way of applying functions to esoteric data structures. In the case of the PHP examples we defined earlier, all you have to do is lift the structure in question to become a functor. Once the structure is *functor-ized*, you can apply structure-agnostic functions to the contained data and the functor will handle pulling the correct value out of the structure.

Applicatives

Now that we have mastered the ins and outs of functors, we can move onto a slightly more complex type called an applicative. Whereas functors applied a function to a wrapped value, applicatives apply a wrapped function to a wrapped value. It may sound pretty crazy, but it's actually relatively simple.

Similar to the functors, we will need to write some code to unpack the wrapped function before we can apply it to the value. There is, of course, no special PHP syntax to handle this, so we will need some boilerplate handling code to have the same effect. Once again, let us begin by implementing an interface for applicatives:

```
interface ApplicativeInterface {
    /**
     * Defines how amap() should deal with this data type
     * @param callable $function
     */
    public function __invoke();
}
```

Also, we need the beginnings of our Applicative type class, which is essentially a nice simple container for the function we wish to wrap up.

Listing 6.7
```
01. class Applicative implements ApplicativeInterface {
02.     protected $function;
03.
04.     public function __construct($function) {
05.         $this->set($function);
06.     }
07.
08.     public function set($function) {
09.         $this->function = $function;
10.     }
11.
12.     public function get() {
13.         return $this->function;
14.     }
15.
16.     public function __invoke() {
17.         if (func_get_arg(0) instanceOf ApplicativeInterface) {
18.             $function = $this->get();
19.
20.             foreach (func_get_args() as $arg) {
21.                 if ($arg instanceOf ApplicativeInterface) {
22.                     $function = compose($function, $arg->get());
23.                 }
24.             }
25.
26.             return new static($function);
27.         } else {
28.             return call_user_func_array($this->get(),
29.                 func_get_args());
30.         }
31.     }
32. }
```

The __invoke() method in Applicative class gives Applicative the equivalent of fmap(), called amap() allowing it to apply its wrapped function to the supplied values. You might have missed that unlike functors, applicatives can handle functions which expect multiple parameters!

So here you can see the contortions that are required to support composition of applicatives and multiple parameters in PHP, but take a moment to read through it, and it should start to make sense.

The first case `__invoke()` handles is the composition of `Applicative` instances into one super `Applicative`. In the second case, we are applying the function wrapped in `Applicative` (`$this->function` in the example) to an array of supplied parameters. The next step is to define the `amap()` function itself so we can actually begin using the `Applicative` type class.

Listing 6.8
```
01. class NotAnApplicativeException extends \Exception {}
02.
03. function amap($applicative) {
04.     $func_name = __FUNCTION__;
05.     $params = array_slice(func_get_args(), 1);
06.
07.     if (is_array($applicative)) {
08.         return array_map(function($actual_applicative)
09.             use ($func_name, $params) {
10.                 array_unshift($params, $actual_applicative);
11.                 return call_user_func_array($func_name, $params);
12.             }, $applicative);
13.     }
14.
15.     if ($applicative instanceOf ApplicativeInterface) {
16.         return call_user_func_array($applicative, $params);
17.     } else {
18.         throw new NotAnApplicativeException($func_name
19.             . ' must be called with an applicative');
20.     }
21. }
```

It is far more complicated than `fmap()`, as you might expect, so I will work through it step-by-step to describe what's happening.

First, it gets its own function name and stores it into a variable for later use. It's also grabbing all the parameters passed to the function except for the first one. Here comes some more good news, `amap()` can apply more than one `Applicative` to the parameters! All you have to do is pass in an array of `Applicatives` as the first parameter to `amap()`, and it will handle the rest. This is why you can see it iterating over an array using `array_map()` before indirectly calling itself.

Next up, is the code to handle the actual call against the `Applicative::__invoke()` method, which is sitting inside a check against the `ApplicativeInterface` to ensure the correct type is being passed in. As you can see, all the parameters for the `amap()` function are passed into the `Applicative` to be applied against the contained function. This means if you are passing in three parameters, then the function wrapped in `Applicative` should be able to handle three parameters. If you do not supply the correct number of arguments, then a PHP error will be triggered. Unfortunately, this is where our PHP emulation of applicative functionality is a little flaky.

Let's review the applicative laws and attempt to verify our implementations against them. I will only attempt to prove two of the laws here as the other two, seen below, are difficult and complex to emulate in PHP.

```
pure (.) <*> u <*> v <*> w = u <*> (v <*> w)
u <*> pure y = pure ($ y) <*> u
```

Fortunately, we can create enough of an applicative for demonstration purposes and to convey the ideas required here.

The first law is equivalent to that which we saw earlier for functors `pure id <*> v = v`, which translates to the following PHP code further clarified in Figure 6.3, Figure 6.4, and Figure 6.5:

```
$id = function($value) {
    return $value;
};
$v = new Just(2);
```

Figure 6.3: Creating a New Just Context

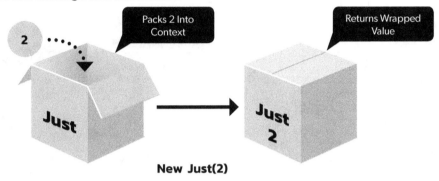

New Just(2)

```
$app_id = new Applicative($id); // pure id
```

Figure 6.4: Inserting a Function into an Applicative Context

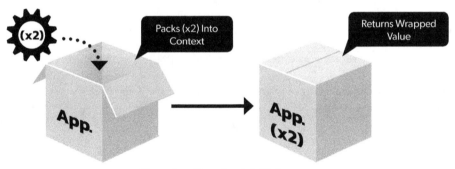

New Applicative((x2))

```
$result = amap($app_id, $v); // <*> v
// $result = Just(2);
// So $result === $v thus proving the law
```

Figure 6.5: Mapping the applicative

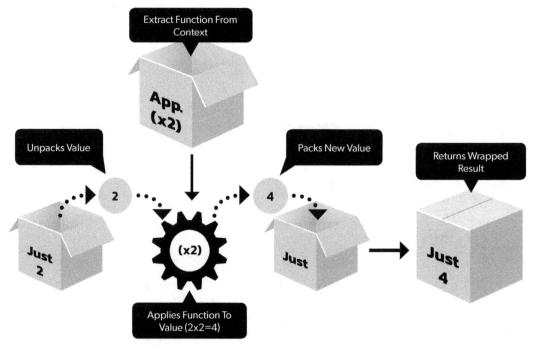

From the result, we can infer that calling the $id()$ function after it has been packed up into an Applicative context against $v will yield $v, and we have therefore proven the first identity law. Much like with the functor example earlier, this ensures packing a function into a context and applying it using amap() does not affect the returned value. It is the responsibility of the function being applied to change the value.

Next up is a check of homomorphism by checking adherence to pure f <*> pure x = pure (f x), which roughly translates as Listing 6.9.

Listing 6.9

```
01. $f = function($value) {
02.     return $value + 1;
03. };
04.
05. $x = function($value) {
06.     return $value + 2;
07. };
08.
09. $pure_f = new Applicative($f); // pure f
10. $pure_x = new Applicative($x); // pure x
11. $result = amap($pure_f, $pure_x); // pure f <*> pure x
12. // $result = Applicative();
13. $pure_fx = new Applicative(function($value) use ($f, $x) {
14.     return $f($x($value));
15. }); // pure (f x)
```

Continued Next Page

```
16.
17. // $pure_fx = Applicative();
18. // $pure_fx should === $result
19. $result(1); // 4
20. $pure_fx(1); // 4
```

The PHP emulation of Applicative does appear to meet this law from the outside, but it is important to note the shape of the context differs between them even though the result is the same.

So to wrap up, if you will pardon the pun, applicatives are like functors on steroids—they pack an extra punch! Functors allow you to apply a function to a value wrapped up in a context, but applicatives can also apply a wrapped function to one or more wrapped values.

Monads

Extending this idea further, you approach the concept of monads. With an understanding of functors and applicatives, you should be able to pick up on the internal operations of a monad more easily, so if you do not have a good grasp on those concepts yet, then I recommend you review them before continuing here.

Monads can be a difficult concept to approach, and the three associated laws only help to deepen the misunderstanding surrounding them. To ease the learning curve, I am going to forgo the formalities and focus on the results. This may not be purely functional code, but the idea is to get you on the way to understanding monads. To begin with, let's address the elephant in the room. The reason most often cited for using a monad is you can maintain state, but it is just one benefit. They also provide a repeatable way to use functions that, at the outset, are incompatible with each other.

Monads may not necessarily be as useful in PHP when compared to purely functional languages. In PHP, there are other ways of handling the problems monads address with better support from the language. Just because it does not necessarily directly translate to a real world use case, however, does not mean it should not be explored and learned about using a familiar programming language. It's a somewhat hidden secret that any language having closures and anonymous functions can produce monads!

The intention of covering monads is to, hopefully, build emulations which will help you to understand similar concepts in functional languages should you wish to explore them. Who knows, you might even find them really useful in a PHP project at some point anyway.

With the disclaimer out of the way, let's dig in and review the core principles which define a monad. There are three universal mathematical laws, but we will address those later as they make it harder to grasp the concepts. A monad is a design pattern where a function returns a wrapped value when fed a wrapped value, which sounds just like the functors or applicatives we have already seen, but there is a gimmick or two, of course.

Where a functor or an applicative will return the result of a function application by repackaging it into the same context, there is no such rule to constrain our new friend the monad. It can take a function which returns a different context and wrestle it into submission. Not only will it apply this function, but the monadic nature of the construct will assist in chaining up functions to be applied to the wrapped value.

Monads do not actually manipulate any of the values in the container as this is the job of the functions you ask it to apply. Just like an applicative, it just knows how to apply the supplied function, but does not actually know or define any of the mutating logic.

For the purposes of simplicity, we must keep in mind the following guidelines while constructing any monad in PHP. A monad maintains a container—an example of a container we have already seen is the Just functor we defined earlier.

In addition, a monad defines two functions allowing us to manipulate the protected container. The first of which is a function to inject a value into the aforementioned container. In Haskell, this is defined as `return`, but we are going to call it `pack()` as it describes the action more clearly to my mind as we are packing the value into a container.

Finally, when we want to apply a function to the values stored in the container, we are going use a method called `map()`, which is the equivalent of Haskell's `bind()`.

Now you have a basic description of what a monad is and its various constituent parts. All monads define these basics, but of course, each has their own implementation details which may expose various other methods for consumption.

Setup a Monad Structure

The monad structure must first be defined so we have a collection of base functionality to assist with the production of monads. Much like with the `Functor` and `Applicative` before it we will define an interface for the `Monad` first.

```
interface MonadInterface {
    public function __construct($value);
    public static function pack($value);
    public function map(callable $function);
}
```

The `MonadInterface` sketches out the two most important aspects of a monad with the `pack()` and `map()` methods representing the only uniform way to communicate with any monad. We can now go ahead and define a base abstract `Monad` class for other monads to extend. If the developer so wishes though they can always implement another abstract for collections so long as he or she implements the `MonadInterface`.

Listing 6.10
```
01. abstract class Monad implements MonadInterface
02. {
03.     protected $container = null;
04.
05.     public function __construct($value) {
06.         $this->container = $value;
07.     }
08.
09.     public static function pack($value) {
10.         return new static($value);
11.     }
12.
13.     public function map(callable $function) {
14.         return $function($this->container);
15.     }
16. }
```

The abstract class in Listing 6.8 implements a container class property which will be used to store the value passed to it internally. More importantly it describes a base set of instructions for how both pack() and map() should behave.

Figure 6.6: Only::pack() in Action

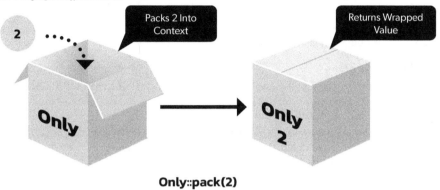

Only::pack(2)

Calling pack() will return a new instance of the monad with the supplied value wrapped up into it—see Figure 6.6. This is completed by passing the value to the constructor of the new instance and this is why the MonadInterface specified the constructor method as well.

Figure 6.7: map() Facilitating Function Application

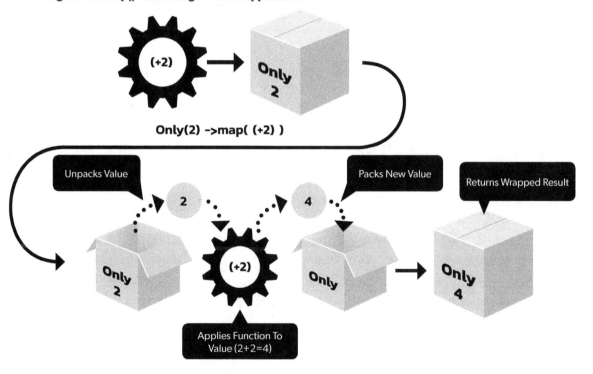

In the case of map() the definition is again fairly simple although it makes use of the callable type annotation to indicate that only items callable as functions should be passed in. It will then opaquely apply the supplied function ($function) to the value previously pack()ed into the monad and return the result—see Figure 6.7.

Functions passed to the map() method of Monad are given access to the container's contents, and it is important they not be allowed to leak any values beyond these walls. This means the $function must wrap up the result of its computation in a monad.

Your First Monad

Confusing? I'll wager you are still scratching your head, so let's look at some code and check out a monad in action. We are going to redefine the Just functor from earlier as a monad in its own right—to prevent a name collision, we will call it Only as it only contains a simple value.

The example below is quite a succinct piece of code thanks to the Monad abstract class we defined earlier handling most of its needs by default. The only method we choose to add here is get() so we actually have a chance of extracting values back out of a monad!

```
class Only extends Monad
{
    public function get() {
        return $this->container;
    }
}
```

Believe it or not, you have defined your first, admittedly very simple, monad! Remember those pesky laws I mentioned? Let's verify our Only monad against them.

The Three Monadic Laws

Firstly, executing map() on a freshly wrapped value (pack()) must yield the same result as giving the value directly to the function you are applying. To make this a little clearer, imagine we have two functions $x() and $y() which accept a value, process it, and pass back a wrapped computation.

```
$x = function($value) {
    return Only::pack($value + 2);
};

$y = function($value) {
    return Only::pack($value * 5);
};
```

Keeping the first law in mind, pack() is a left identity for map(), which can be programmatically defined as:

```
Only::pack(2)->map($x);
```

This must have the same result as directly applying the function to the same value unwrapped.

```
$x(2);
```

Second, passing in a function which does not operate on the supplied value, but only applies pack() to it must return precisely the same values bound up in a monad. This means pack() is a right identity for map().

```
$only = Only::pack(2);
$only_applied = $only->map(function($value) {
  return Only::pack($value);
});
// $only === $only_applied
```

This is a basic protection against pack() or map() affecting the value as nothing should change the result, except for the anonymous function itself.

Third, nesting map() calls must produce the same result as when they are called sequentially. To put this another way, if you chain calls to map(), you should get the same result as calling them in a nested function. This can be illustrated with PHP code like:

```
$only = Only::pack(2)->map($x)->map($y);
```

Which must be functionally equivalent to:

```
$only = Only::pack(2)->map(function($value) use ($x, $y) {
  return $x($value)->map(function($value) use ($y) {
    return $y($value);
  });
});
```

Hopefully, you have endured the pseudocode unscathed and have come out the other side understanding the basics of the three laws for creating a bona fide monad. Now all that remains is to test our Only monad against these laws to verify its status as a genuine monad.

To prove the first law, the variables $a and $b in the following code must contain the same result.

```
$a = Only::pack(2)->map($x); // Only(4)
$b = $x(2); // Only(4)
```

As you can see, they both contain the same result: an integer of 4, which proves law one!

On to law two; we must prove a function returns an instance of Only with:

```
$c = Only::pack(2); // Only(2)
$d = $c->map(function($value) {
  return Only::pack($value);
}); // Only(2)
```

In this case, both $c and $d should contain the same wrapped value in the same shaped context. In the case of Only, we have proven they definitely do.

So now, we get to the third and final law our monad must adhere to—the following code demonstrates being called sequentially is the same as being called in a nested manner.

```
$only = Only::pack(2);
$e = $only->map($x)->map($y); // Only(20)
$f = $only->map(function($value) use ($x, $y) {
  return $x($value)->map(function($value) use ($y) {
    return $y($value);
  });
}); // Only(20)
```

Thankfully, our Only monad has also proven itself a match for the third law, and we have successfully proven you have written your first monad. Congratulations!

Maybe We Can Have a Second Monad

With the basics down pat, it is time to move onto something more challenging and useful. As you have already seen the php-option library in *Handling Your NULLs*, we will introduce a monad-style solution to the same concepts.

However, first, let's briefly review the issue we are trying to solve. When coding, it is common to make requests to external resources—such as databases or files—which may or may not return a result.

```php
$sth = $pdo->prepare("SELECT * FROM umuntu");
$sth->execute();
$row = $sth->fetch(PDO::FETCH_LAZY);
echo 'Name: ';

if ($row) {
    echo $row->ibizo . ' (verified)';
} else {
    echo 'Unknown';
}
```

The preceding code illustrates a simple database query to fetch a person's first name from the person table. If there is no result, then it simply prints out "Name: Unknown", but if a name is found, then it should append the label "(verified)" to the person's name, rendering "Name: Marion (verified)". It becomes very tiresome to always check the return values of each call to a resource which may or may not exist, and it is much easier to always assume it does. In Haskell, this is known as the `Maybe` monad, and we will simulate it here in PHP.

Once again, the `Maybe` monad is essentially a simple container much like the `Only` monad we defined earlier.

To this end we will add a couple of custom methods to form the basis of a `Maybe` construct, but first, let us run through the base methods forming Listing 6.11.

Listing 6.11

```php
01. class Maybe extends Monad
02. {
03.     public function mapAndPack(callable $function) {
04.         return $this->isNothing() ?
05.             $this :
06.             static::pack($this->map($function));
07.     }
08.
09.     public function isNothing() {
10.         return (null === $this->container);
11.     }
12.
13.     public function getOrElse($default) {
14.         return $this->isNothing() ?
15.             $default :
16.             $this->container;
17.     }
18.
19.     public function get() {
20.         return $this->container;
21.     }
22. }
```

As the `pack()` method is not overridden and it is therefore the same as the one we already used for `Only` from `Monad`, let us just skip over that and concentrate on the minor customizations in the wrapper around `map()`—`mapAndPack()`. If the result is nothing (`isNothing()` will be defined shortly), then the monad simply returns itself without applying the supplied function. Should there be a genuine value in the container, the function will be applied and the new value will be returned wrapped up in a `Maybe` context.

The `isNothing()` method itself simply checks if the contained value is null and returns a Boolean depending on its state.

`Maybe` gets more interesting once you define the `getOrElse()` method as it allows you to return a default value if the container is empty or the contained value if there is one. To illustrate this functionality in action, here is the imperative example implemented using the `Maybe` monad instead of an imperative `if else`.

```
$sth = $pdo->prepare("SELECT * FROM umuntu");
$sth->execute();
$row = $sth->fetch(PDO::FETCH_LAZY);
$verify_names = function($value) {
  return $value->ibizo . ' (verified)';
};
echo 'Name: ' . Maybe::pack($row)->
  mapAndPack($verify_names)->
  getOrElse('Unknown');
```

Just as in the imperative example, when there is no row available, this code will echo "Name: Unknown". If there is a record, it will display "Name: Marion (verified)". The advantage of using the monad in this case is it could be chained with other function applications, the code to add the verified label can be easily reused elsewhere, and the code is arguably easier to read and simpler to write.

Writer Monad

When working with pure PHP functions, it can be useful to add some debugging information to them for logging purposes. As we are inside a pure function, we must not attempt to set state or cause any side effects such as printing directly to screen. All of our functions should pass their output as return values. You need a construct to add flexibility to your functions—the `Writer` monad.

The `Writer` monad allows you to write out to screen, disk, memory, etc. while also maintaining the method chain and common interface. To show this in action, we will need at least two simple functions we can apply to the `Writer` monad.

Our first function is a simple method, stripping non-alpha characters from a string:

```
$strip = function($x) {
  return preg_replace('/[^a-z]/i', '', $x);
};
```

Let us apply this function to an actual value so we can see it in action:

```
$str = 'Akl;^(&^EW(&W)Ehdbnjd33445454nbgfwoqf';
echo $strip($str); // AklEWWEhdbnjdnbgfwoqf
```

To compliment this functionality, the second function below will convert the supplied string to base 64.

```
$str = 'AklEWWEhdbnjdnbgfwoqf';
$base64 = function($x) {
  return base64_encode($x);
};
echo $base64($str); // QWtsRVdXRWhkYm5qZG5iZ2Z3b3Fm
```

Both of these functions take the same number of arguments and return the same value type, which makes them composable functions without further modification. The return value of one function can be passed directly into the other as an argument. To demonstrate this ability, we must use the `compose()` function we defined earlier.

```
$strip_base64 = compose($strip, $base64);
echo $strip_base64($str); // QWtsRVdXRWhkYm55qZG5iZ2Z3b3Fm
```

As you can see, the return value is as expected—the same as if you had called `echo $base64($strip($str))`. Suppose for a moment we did not know that, and we were curious to know which function was being applied to `$str` first. To prove our hypothesis, we can use logging to determine the call order of the functions.

The first thing you would normally do in PHP is to add statements printing out a message to screen from each function, but as I mentioned before, that is cheating and breaks pure functions! For this example, you are to wipe that knowledge from your mind. We will add logging strings as return values from the functions instead, see Listing 6.12.

Listing 6.12
```
23. $strip = function($x) {
24.    return array(
25.        preg_replace('/[^a-z]/i', '', $x),
26.        'Non-alphas stripped from string',
27.    );
28. };
29.
30. $base64 = function($x) {
31.    return array(
32.        base64_encode($x),
33.        'Encoding the string to base64',
34.    );
35. };
```

Now that we have logging in place, we can compose the functions again and try the same string manipulations again.

```
$strip_base64 = compose($strip, $base64);
echo $strip_base64($str);
```

Unfortunately, the logging has broken our function composition and triggers a PHP error.

```
PHP Warning: base64_encode() expects parameter 1 to be
   string, array given
```

Our functions only accept one string parameter, and we are now trying to stuff an array into one of them. This is what you expect PHP to do, but it is not what we want.

Immediately, you are probably thinking of ways to work around this annoyance. At least one method revolves around modifying the second function (`$base64`) to accept an array as its first parameter, but this would change the function's signature. It would also mean you would not be able to compose the functions in reverse order.

The next option you are probably thinking about is to write a wrapping function calling both functions internally and combining the results. It will work, but it is not as flexible as it could be—think again of the possible need to reverse the composition in the future or other methods of reuse.

Instead, let's write a higher order compose function specifically for handling these function signatures. It will accept the two string functions we created earlier as arguments and return a composed function.

Listing 6.13

```
01. $compose_log = function($f, $g) {
02.     return function($x) use($f, $g) {
03.         $fx = $f($x);
04.         $y  = $fx[0]; // AklEWWEhdbnjdnbgfwoqf
05.         $s  = $fx[1]; // Non-alphas stripped from string
06.         $gy = $g($y);
07.         $z  = $gy[0]; // QWtsRVdXRWhkYm5qZG5iZ2Z3b3Fm
08.         $t  = $gy[1]; // Encoding the string to base64
09.         return array($z, $s . $t);
10.     };
11. };
12. $strip_base64 = $compose_log($strip, $base64);
13. $j = $strip_base64($str);
14. // array(
15. //     "QWtsRVdXRWhkYm5qZG5iZ2Z3b3Fm",
16. //     "Non-alphas stripped from stringEncoding the string to
17. //         base64"
18. // )
```

This can be improved still further, however, by converting or lifting our functions to interoperable debug functions rather than writing custom composing functions.

Essentially, the function signature of the original function was:

```
f:String = String
```

With our most recent modifications, we have created:

```
f:String = [String, String]
```

However, we want to convert them so the signature changes to:

```
f:[String, String] = [String, String]
```

In this way, it is possible to use the universal compose() function rather than some custom logic each time to compose individual cases.

This is where we introduce the naming conventions we used in the Only and Maybe monads we have already seen. The first order of business is lifting the value passed into each function so it is an array. By default, the log is set to an empty string.

Listing 6.14

```
01. class Writer extends Monad {
02.     public static function lift($value, $log = '') {
03.         return static::pack(array($value, $log));
04.     }
05.     public function map(callable $f) {
06.         $x = $this->container[0];
07.         $s = $this->container[1];
08.         $fx = $f($x);
09.         $y = $fx[0];
10.         $t = $fx[1];
11.         return static::lift($y, $s . $t);
12.     }
13. }
```

Lifting the functions to accept an array as a parameter and then applying it is the job of the map() method. Now let's see our latest monad in action by wrapping our string in a new Writer monad.

```
$Wstr = Writer::lift($str);
// Writer(
//     array(
//         "Akl;^(&^EW(&W)Ehdbnjd33445454nbgfwoqf",
//         ""
//     )
// )
```

To use our monad, we need to apply a function to it, so let's start with $strip() again:

```
$Wstr2 = $Wstr->map($strip);
// Writer(
//     array(
//         "AklEWWEhdbnjdnbgfwoqf",
//         "Non-alphas stripped from string"
//     )
// )
```

Finally for the pièce de résistance, we can chain our call to $base64() onto the result from $strip():

```
$Wstr3 = $Wstr2->map($base64);
// Writer(
//     array(
//         "QWtsRVdXRWhkYm5qZG5iZ2Z3b3Fm",
//         "Non-alphas stripped from stringEncoding the string
//             to base64"
//     )
// )
```

As you can clearly see from the results, we now have a Writer monad containing exactly the same values we achieved via our custom composition function ($compose_log()). From here, you have the tools to create new monads for various other pieces of functionality. My suggestion is the Reader and State monads are probably the next most useful, so I would recommend starting there.

Chapter

7

Implementing the Theory

"You'd like to be able to write a contract for a function like: 'you give me arguments that are bigger than zero and I will give you a result that is smaller than zero."

—Simon Peyton Jones (Computer scientist, *@simonpj0*)

IP Address Restriction

As is customary when introducing a new topic, the first example will be kept simple both in terms of the problem it is solving and the code which is implemented. While the code may never make it into production, it does provide a good starting point. Blocking access to users who do not appear in an IP address white list can be done in a number of ways with PHP. This example will take the approach of encoding it in the shortest amount of code possible in PHP, to my knowledge.

We need an IP v4 address to represent the address of the website user for the following examples. To make the code more easily adaptable to a web server environment as opposed to the command line the simplest way of doing this is to override $_SERVER['REMOTE_ADDR'] with a static IP address of our choosing. Simply remove this line when running this code via web server to check the actual user's IP address:

```
$_SERVER['REMOTE_ADDR'] = '86.72.216.14';
```

To begin with the white list of IP addresses must be defined to have something to check against:

```
$allowable_ips = [
   '8.8.8.8',
   '192.168.0.125',
   '127.0.0.1',
   '86.72.216.14',
];
```

Verifying the IP addresses is quite simple by making use of `array_filter()`. The callback function will check if the users IP address matches any of those in the white list.

Array filter will be executed against the IP address white list so the function should accept on IP address as an argument, as in:

```
array_filter($allowable_ips, function($ip) {
   return $ip == $_SERVER['REMOTE_ADDR'];
}) ?: die('Denied.');
```

Finally the code applies a short ternary conditional to the result of the `array_filter()`. This means if the list is empty then there was no match and the user should be denied access which is currently implemented with a simple `die()`. If the array contains something, then there was a match and the user should be allowed to continue so here the code simply does nothing and continues.

Wouldn't it be nice to be able to verify against partial IP addresses too?

This would allow the code to be used against sub-nets and not just full IP addresses. In the case of a simple office intranet we could then allow the whole office in, but be more explicit with their home addresses. After all, we don't want any old person with the same internet service provider getting in!

To this end we will add a couple of partial IP addresses to the white list:

```
$allowable_ips += [
   '192.168.0.',
   '86.',
];
```

The `array_filter` must also be changed to allow it to handle matching these new partial IP addresses against the users IP address.

```
array_filter($allowable_ips, function($ip) {
   return $ip == substr($_SERVER['REMOTE_ADDR'],
                        0, strlen($ip));
}) ?: die('Denied.');
```

In order to handle partial IP addresses the function takes a substring (same length as the white list value) of the current user's IP address and compares it against the white list value. A small complication, but one that is easy to add.

So there you have it, a simple IP v4 white list checking script in three lines of code! OK, so you probably aren't going to want to put this into production, but it does serve as a nice simple self-contained example, albeit with side effects (`die()`).

Functional Primitives

The Setup

Let's run through a few examples of how these features could potentially be combined to assist in reporting for a vehicle repair business. Please see the code sample below for the base set of data all of these operations will be working upon.

Listing 7.1

```
01. // Odometer: distance covered by a vehicle in miles or
02. //     kilometres
03. // Rego: Vehicle registration or plate number
04. // Hours: Time spent working on the vehicle
05. // Parts cost: Charge to the customer for the cost of parts
06.
07. $service_logs = [
08.     ['rego' => 'DG44-001', 'odometer' => 91234,
09.         'hours' => 0.36, 'parts_cost' => 31.99],
10.     ['rego' => 'LJ32-091', 'odometer' => 7986,
11.         'hours' => 1, 'parts_cost' => 278.54],
12.     ['rego' => 'DG44-001', 'odometer' => 58709,
13.         'hours' => 3, 'parts_cost' => 1002.29],
14.     ['rego' => 'DG44-001', 'odometer' => 23487,
15.         'hours' => 10, 'parts_cost' => 3932.96],
16. ];
17.
18. $charge_per_hour = 120;
19. $overhead_per_hour = 10;
```

The initial setup is simple enough, so let's go ahead and pull in the vendor autoloader from Composer and the functional-php namespace:

```
require_once 'vendor/autoload.php';

use Functional as F;
```

Another small piece of housekeeping also needs to be completed so we can make a more functional `uasort()` available to our program. Unfortunately, PHP edits the array in place and does not return the sorted array, but a Boolean value. This, of course, violates our pact to ensure all data in our functional program is immutable, so this wrapping function goes part of the way to rectifying it.

```
function functional_sort($collection, $callback) {
    uasort($collection, $callback);
    return $collection;
}
```

Sort and Pluck

Let's keep it simple for the first example by pulling out the highest vehicle mileage in the records. A handy hint for you when reading nested function calls like this is it's best to read from the inside out.

```
$highest_odometer_reading = F\first(
    functional_sort(
        F\pluck($service_logs, 'odometer'),
        function($a, $b) {
            return ($a < $b);
        }
    )
);
```

First, F\pluck() is called to return an array of the mileage elements from the service logs. At this point, the value the program is operating on becomes:

```
[ 91234, 7986, 58709, 23487 ];
```

This functionality is available in PHP 5.5 under the name array_column() as the related RFC[1] was voted through.

However, let's get back to our odometer reading example. The next function to operate on the service logs is a sorting algorithm using the custom functional_sort() which we defined earlier. Then finally, F\first() grabs the top record off the stack and assigns the value 91234 to the $highest_odometer_reading variable.

Reduction

Cutting the data another way makes it possible to calculate the total profit the garage has made on the service work it has performed. Again, take a look at the first code sample in this chapter for the origin of the $charge_per_hour and $overhead_per_hour variables used in the algorithm closure.

```
$profit = F\reduce_left(
    $service_logs,
    function($value, $index, $collection, $result)
        use ($charge_per_hour, $overhead_per_hour) {
        return $result +
            ($value['hours'] * $charge_per_hour) -
            ($value['hours'] * $overhead_per_hour) +
            $value['parts_cost'];
    }
);
```

The code is simply using a reduce to go through each service record, calculating the profit on each job and adding it to the accumulating $result variable. When the value is finally assigned to $profit, it is a single float of 6825.38. You may have noticed this function does not take into account the cost to the business of the parts (in the example, parts_cost is the cost for the customer)–this is just to simplify the example code.

The F\reduce_left() function is functionally equivalent to PHP's native array_reduce(), except like the rest of functional-php, it can operate on objects implementing Traversable. The library also makes F\reduce_right() available with the difference being it begins reducing from the last element in the collection whereas F\reduce_left() begins with the first element in the collection.

[1]   Array Column RFC: https://wiki.php.net/rfc/array_column

It is possible to make some improvements to the program by factoring out the profit calculation code into a separate closure which can be reused.

```
$calculate_profit = function($hours, $parts_cost)
  use ($charge_per_hour, $overhead_per_hour) {
  return ($hours * $charge_per_hour) -
    ($hours * $overhead_per_hour) +
    $parts_cost;
};
```

Now we can tighten up the collection processing functionality as well by using three functions from functional-php.

```
$profit2 = F\sum(
  F\zip(
    F\pluck($service_logs, 'hours'),
    F\pluck($service_logs, 'parts_cost'),
    $calculate_profit
  )
);
```

Beginning with the inner functions first and working outwards, F\pluck() is used to pull the hours and parts_cost elements from each service log record. F\zip() is then employed to combine the two resulting arrays using the $calculate_profit closure as the combining operation and returns an array containing the profit subtotal for every service log record. These subtotals are then totaled up into one final profit total, which is then returned as a float from F\sum() and assigned to $profit2.

Filtering with Partials

Often, customers will want to obtain a complete list of the service history for their vehicle or a vehicle they have recently purchased. With the assistance of some filtering combined with a sorting algorithm, it is possible to return an array of service logs ordered by odometer reading for a particular vehicle registration number.

```
function get_by_rego($service_logs, $rego) {
  return functional_sort(
    F\filter($service_logs, function($value) use ($rego) {
      return ($rego == $value['rego']);
    }),
    function($a, $b) {
      return ($a['odometer'] > $b['odometer']);
    }
  );
}
```

Initially, the service logs are filtered down to only those matching the vehicle registration which has been passed in using F\filter() with a callback closure function. The resulting array is then ordered by each service record's odometer reading with an ascending sort.

To make it easier to use this function, we can bind the `$service_logs` variable to the function using the React/Partial function application library.

```
use React\Partial;

$get_by_rego = Partial\bind('get_by_rego', $service_logs,
  Partial\ ());
```

It is then possible to easily obtain the records for a vehicle registration number by calling `$get_by_rego()`.

```
$result = $get_by_rego('DG44-001');

// array(
//    array("rego" => "DG44-001", "odometer" => 23487,
//          "hours" => 10, "parts_cost" => 3932.96),
//    array("rego" => "DG44-001", "odometer" => 58709,
//          "hours" => 3, "parts_cost" => 1002.29),
//    array("rego" => "DG44-001", "odometer" => 91234,
//          "hours" => 0.36, "parts_cost" => 31.99)
// )
```

This could also be implemented using functional-php's `F\group()` function to first group all the records by a vehicle registration number instead of `F\filter()`, but this would be less efficient in terms of memory usage as the array would be much larger.

From these highly contrived examples, you can see some of the ways functional primitives and higher order functions can be combined to achieve business goals. They also highlight the advantages of keeping functions simple and confined to answering one problem each, thereby facilitating their eventual combined use and re-use.

A Domain Specific Language in PHP

This may seem like an unlikely application for the PHP language given its relatively inflexible nature. You can't define your own keywords and there are no infix operators for example. On top of this there are no decent combinators available!

Simple languages can be expressed in terms of PHP functions though, as this example implementing HTML will demonstrate. HTML was chosen for the DSL (Domain Specific Language) as the rules should be familiar to all PHP developers. In keeping with the theme of ensuring simplicity this example will only implement a small subset of HTML. There will be just enough to demonstrate the concept and allow you to see how it maps functions to the varying HTML requirements.

To make things easier, you will notice the use of objects where appropriate in this example code. These objects have been implemented in an almost functional style with no global state changes and they are not really treated as classes in the object oriented sense. That is to say, the objects are merely being consumed as typed collections. This allows our code to make assumptions about what it is being passed, unlike if it were passed an array, for instance. It's a way to emulate a very basic type system, a feature of many functional programming languages.

Functional programming is not necessarily the nemesis of object-oriented code, but it does provide a compelling alternative. Well written object-oriented code can almost look functional as it shares some of the fundamental concepts. Keep things dedicated, reusable, and with an easily implementable interface.

Onto the example itself where HTML is the domain we wish to convert into a language in PHP.

Before writing any code it is helpful to plan how the API will look once it is completed. A simple way of doing this is to list out the namespaces you intend to create. For HTML this could look something like the following list of namespaces:

- \FpPhp\Utils
- \FpPhp\Html\Html4
- \FpPhp\Html\Html5

Then, beneath each namespace it becomes easier to list out the functions which might be needed. In the case of the current example, this might look something like the following namespace grouped list of functions:

- \FpPhp\Utils
  - ensure_array
- \FpPhp\Html\Html4
  - div
  - a
- \FpPhp\Html\Html5
  - section
  - aside

While there are inevitably more functions which could be added to the list, for the sake of brevity only those to be implemented in the example are included here.

I normally do these sketches of functionality in code where I define the namespace and include function stubs underneath them. This way, they are easy to move around and some of the work is already completed when it comes to implementation. Alongside this I also begin producing unit tests for the functions I am adding to the namespaces. This allows me to easily ensure the functions are producing the results I expect as I develop and it has the added benefit that refactors can be easier.

To begin we will create the Utils namespace which will contain functions we might like to reuse or that are not specifically to do with producing HTML.

Listing 7.2
```
01. namespace FpPhp\Utils
02. {
03.     /**
04.      * Force a variable to be an array
05.      * @param mixed $array
06.      * @return array
07.      */
08.     function ensure_array($array) {
09.         return is_array($array) ?
10.                 $array :
11.                 [ $array ];
12.     }
13. }
```

For this particular project we only require a simple function that given a value will ensure it is an array and wrap it in an array if it is not: ensure_array().

The next namespace will be Html4, which implements the tags div and a in our domain specific language.

Listing 7.3

```
01. namespace FpPhp\Html\Html4
02. {
03.     use \FpPhp\Html as H;
04.     /**
05.      * Create a DIV tag
06.      * @param string $content
07.      * @param array $attrs Array of Attribute instances
08.      * /@return string
09.      */
10.     function div($content, array $attrs = []) {
11.         return H\tag('div', $content, $attrs);
12.     }
13.
14.     /**
15.      * Create an A tag
16.      * @param string $content
17.      * @param array $attrs Array of Attribute instances
18.      * @return string
19.      */
20.     function a($content, array $attrs = []) {
21.         return H\tag('a', $content, $attrs);
22.     }
23. }
```

As you can see in Listing 7.3 it actually uses another namespace \FpPhp\Html and calls methods within it for both the div() and a() functions. This underlying namespace will contain functions which Html4 and Html5 will make use of when producing their respective tags. The tag functions themselves (a() and div()) are actually very simple and all work is passed off to the library of functions in \FpPhp\Html.

The next step is to create that underlying library of functions—oh, and one class to hold the values of HTML tag attributes (Attribute). First, we will implement the \FpPhp\Html namespace so we can begin to add functions to it:

```
namespace FpPhp\Html {
    use FpPhp\Utils as U;
}
```

Into the namespace we will first add a simple class to act as the container for an HTML attribute (class, href, style, etc.). It is necessary to use a class here as we want to type check against attribute values later on and it serves as a nice way of preprocessing and storing the structured data.

Listing 7.4

```
01. /**
02.  * Represents an HTML attribute
03.  */
04. class Attribute
05. {
06.     protected $name = '';
07.     protected $values = [];
08.
09.     public function __construct($name, $values) {
10.         $this->name = $name;
11.         $this->values = U\ensure_array($values);
12.     }
13.
14.     public function name() {
15.         return $this->name;
16.     }
17.
18.     public function values() {
19.         return $this->values;
20.     }
21. }
```

The constructor is the only way of adding data into the structure which effectively creates an immutable structure and it means we can intercept the value. We need the value to be an array so we use the `Utils\ensure_array()` function from Listing 7.2 so any scalar value will be converted into an array element.

Creating a new `Attribute` instance for each attribute is not all that arduous, but like any good programmer we are lazy so we will add a function called `attr()`. This function will act as a factory and ease the process of creating new `Attribute` instances.

```
/**
 * Create a new attribute
 * @param   $name
 * @param array|string|null $values
 * @return \FpPhp\Html\Attribute
 */
function attr($name, $values = null) {
    return new Attribute($name, $values);
}
```

Passing in a name and a value (scalar or array) will return you a new instance of the `Attribute` class containing that information. That's it for the creation of new attributes with this set of code for the domain specific language. Next up we will define the functions which create a new tag and process its associated `Attributes` into an HTML ready string. The `tag()` function will generate a new tag and it is as good a starting point as anywhere.

Listing 7.5

```
01. /**
02.  * Create an HTML tag
03.  * @param string $type
04.  * @param string $content
05.  * @param array $attrs Array of Attribute instances
06.  * @return string
07.  */
08. function tag($type, $content, array $attrs = []) {
09.     return "<$type" . attrs_to_html($attrs) . ">"
10.         . $content . "</$type>";
11. }
```

When supplied a type (section, div, etc.) and some content, the tag() function will produce an HTML tag. So if you were to call it with a type of div and sawubona as the content it would emit <div>sawubona</div>. It's really very simple and this one function makes it easy to create a HTML tag of any type by passing the name in as the type such as div, section or a.

What of the attributes array though? This is where it gets a little more complicated with the processing of the instances of Attribute and we pass this off to another function attrs_to_html() to break the problem down into more focused functions. This is one of the handy features of programming in a stricter functional style as it automatically leaves you with more repurposable functions.

Listing 7.6

```
01. /**
02.  * Take an array of attributes and get them in HTML format
03.  * @param array $attrs Array of Attribute instances
04.  * @return string
05.  */
06. function attrs_to_html(array $attrs) {
07.     return ($attrs) ?
08.         ' ' . implode(' ',
09.             array_map('\FpPhp\Html\attr_to_html', $attrs))
10.         : '';
11. }
```

In Listing 7.7 attrs_to_html() is defined as a function which accepts a single array as input, which should contain instances of Attribute. If the array is not empty, then it will use array_map() to execute a function against each value in the array before imploding the output into a space delimited string. Where $attrs is empty the attrs_to_html() function will simply return an empty string in sympathy. Now, onto the next function attr_to_html(), which is called against each instance of Attribute by attrs_to_html().

Listing 7.7

```
01. /**
02.  * Take an array of attributes and get them in HTML format
03.  * @param array $attrs Array of Attribute instances
04.  * @return string
05.  */
06. function attrs_to_html(array $attrs) {
07.     return ($attrs) ?
08.         ' ' . implode(' ',
09.             array_map('\FpPhp\Html\attr_to_html', $attrs))
10.         : '';
11. }
```

In reality, `attr_to_html()` is another intermediary function which passes the work off to another function called `render_attr()` after imploding the list of attribute values (in the case of `class` HTML attribute these would be the various classes we wish to apply to the tag; `col6 panel-padding round-border` might be the output for example). This imploded list and the attribute name (`class`) would be passed onto `render_attr()` to be converted into an HTML attribute.

Listing 7.8

```
01. /**
02.  * Render an HTML attribute
03.  * @param string $name
04.  * @param string $value
05.  * @return string
06.  */
07. function render_attr($name, $value = null) {
08.     return (
09.         is_null($value) || false === $value || '' === $value)
10.         ? $name
11.         : $name . '="' . esc_html($value) . '"';
12. }
```

Again this is a pretty simple function, but there are a couple of aspects worth pointing out. The reason we must explicitly check for `null`, `false` and an empty string is because some attributes may have a value of `0` so we cannot simply evaluate `return ($value) ?:` as you might initially expect. Supposing the value passed in is empty then it will be added without a value which suits something like `disabled`, `selected` or `checked` on HTML form inputs.

Were there to be an actual value passed through, then it would first be sent to `esc_html()` and then rendered as a quoted HTML attribute. Using the examples from before it would emit `class="col6 panel-padding round-border"` as its return value. The `esc_html()` (Listing 7.9) is a very simple wrapper around PHPs core `htmlspecialchars()` function so all the appropriate flags can be set without fuss in a re-usable fashion.

Listing 7.9

```
01. /**
02.  * HTML escape an string
03.  * @param string $string
04.  */
05. function esc_html($string) {
06.     return htmlspecialchars(
07.         $string,
08.         ENT_HTML5 | ENT_COMPAT | ENT_SUBSTITUTE,
09.         'UTF-8'
10.     );
11. }
```

And that is it for the FpPhp\Html namespace. Before moving onto the FpPhp\Html\Html5 namespace we should probably test the code to make sure it works.

Listing 7.10
```
01. use FpPhp\Html as H,
02.     FpPhp\Html\Html4;
03. $div_tag = Html4\div(
04.     'Ngiyabathanda abantwana bami.',
05.     [
06.         H\attr('class', [ 'red-block', 'title' ]),
07.         H\attr('data-id', 't12345'),
08.     ]
09. );
10. // <div class="red-block title" data-id="t12345">
11. //     Ngiyabathanda abantwana bami.</div>
```

As the div example in Listing 7.10 shows, it is relatively easy to use this naive DSL to produce HTML. By wrapping the tag() function you can quickly add new HTML tags to the language and make use of them through the same universal interface.

To that end, how about we add some more methods for the HTML5 namespace mentioned earlier.

Listing 7.11
```
01. namespace FpPhp\Html\Html5
02. {
03.     use \FpPhp\Html as H;
04.
05.     /**
06.      * Create a section tag
07.      * @param string $content
08.      * @param array $attrs Array of Attribute instances
09.      * @return string
10.      */
11.     function section($content, array $attrs = []) {
12.         return H\tag('section', $content, $attrs);
13.     }
14.
15.     /**
16.      * Create an aside tag
17.      * @param string $content
18.      * @param array $attrs Array of Attribute instances
19.      * @return string
20.      */
21.     function aside($content, array $attrs = []) {
22.         return H\tag('aside', $content, $attrs);
23.     }
24. }
```

Much like the HTML4 examples before it, Listing 7.11 simply adds two new tags to the DSL so you can create `section` and `aside` tags. It would be trivial to implement a `script`, `nav` or `main` tag in either of the namespaces. I find the easiest way to introduce new functionality is to write a unit test along with it—for this book I have been using Sebastian Bergmann's PHPUnit[2]. As I added each new piece of functionality I wrote a unit test first and then produced the new function to pass the test.

As a final example we shall create a short snippet of nested HTML using the domain specific language functions we now have available to use in both the HTML4 and HTML5 namespaces. Listing 7.12 creates a very simple snippet of HTML the describes an article with some navigation beside it.

Listing 7.12

```
01. use FpPhp\Html as H,
02.     FpPhp\Html\Html4,
03.     FpPhp\Html\Html5;
04.
05. $snippet = Html4\div(
06.     Html5\section(
07.         Html4\div(
08.             'Ngiyabathanda abantwana bami.',
09.             [
10.                 H\attr('class', [ 'red-block', 'title' ]),
11.                 H\attr('data-id', 't12345'),
12.             ]
13.         )
14.     ) .
15.     Html5\aside(
16.         Html4\div(
17.             Html4\a('Home', [ H\attr('href', '/') ]) .
18.             Html4\a('Blog', [ H\attr('href', '/blog') ]) .
19.             Html4\a('About', [ H\attr('href', '/about') ]),
20.             [ H\attr('class', 'nav') ]
21.         )
22.     ),
23.     [ H\attr('class', 'wrapper') ]
24. );
25. // <div class="wrapper"><section><div class="red-block title"
26. // data-id="t12345">Ngiyabathanda abantwana bami.</div></section>
27. // <aside><div class="nav"><a href="/">Home</a><a href="/blog">Blog</a>
28. // <a href="/about">About</a></div></aside></div>
```

Hopefully this short run-down gives you an idea of how powerful PHP can be in a functional style and what can be done with a domain specific language in PHP. If you want more opportunities to put this into practice, then you could write a DSL for building a JSON or XML builder or even a language for creating RTF files.

[2] PHPUnit: http://phpunit.de

Chapter

Event Driven Programming

> *"If people do not believe that mathematics is simple, it is only because they do not realize how complicated life is."*
>
> —John von Neumann (Mathematician and Physicist, 1903–1957)

One well-established use of functional-style code is in event-driven programming. If you have written JavaScript code before, you will likely have previous experience with this paradigm. Functions such as `setInterval()` and `onClick()` are just two such examples which make use of an event-driven approach in JavaScript. This is not a method of working PHP easily supports out of the box, but thankfully, there a few extensions and libraries out there to help.

The functional approach of removing and avoiding state is a major advantage when dealing with asynchronous code. Of course, it would also be much more difficult to create such programs if simple functional constructs—such as lambdas and closures—were not available to handle callback duties.

In the PECL repository, there are a number of extensions intended to provide PHP with non-blocking I/O functionality such as libevent, eio, event, and ev. In terms of libraries, there is ReactPHP (you might recognize this name from the partial function application section) and a few other less well known options. For the purposes of demonstration, we will use ReactPHP[1] here as it is easier to install and does not have any additional server requirements like the aforementioned PECL extensions (which are also worth checking out, though!).

[1]   ReactPHP: <u>http://reactphp.org</u>

ReactPHP Installation

Installation is incredibly simple with the help of Composer. After *installing Composer*, in a fresh directory, you can run:

```
composer init --require=react/http:0.3.* -n
composer install
```

Composer will install the ReactPHP components for use in your project.

Getting Started

Just like with earlier examples of Composer installed libraries, you need to add the vendor autoloading to your file (`server.php`) first.

```
require 'vendor/autoload.php';
```

Then, we can get on with the business of setting up a simple web server, which—at its heart—is a long running PHP process. When a request is made to the server, this bubbles up as an event and triggers the actioning callback. If you have previous experience with NodeJS, then this pattern will be very familiar to you.

First, we will define a simple request-handling function that just returns a string.

```
$rh = function($request, $response) {
    $response->writeHead(200, [
        'Content-Type' => 'text/plain'
    ]);
    $response->end("Sakubona, unjani?");
};
```

Next up is the actual web server itself, and the necessary event loop to turn it into a long-running process:

```
$loop = React\EventLoop\Factory::create();
$socket = new React\Socket\Server($loop);
$http = new React\Http\Server($socket, $loop);
```

Finally, we must bind the request handler (`$rh`) to the server (`$http`), set a socket for the server to listen to, and set the event loop in motion.

```
$http->on('request', $rh);
$socket->listen(7355);
$loop->run();
```

The server can now be started on the command line with `php server.php`. You can now access the server on `http://127.0.0.1:7355`, and you will receive a simple plain-text response of `Sakubona, unjani?`.

The library is a high-level abstraction above code which can be written in PHP with the `stream_*()` functions, but if you install `libevent` or `libev`, then it will use their C implementations as faster back ends. The HTTP server we have defined here could be written with pure PHP code:

```
$srv = stream_socket_server('tcp://127.0.0.1:7355');
while ($sh = stream_socket_accept($srv, -1)) {
    fwrite($sh, "HTTP/1.1 200 OK\r\n\r\n");
    fwrite($sh, "Sakubona, unjani?\n");
    fclose($sh);
}
```

It is important to note ReactPHP has added a number of logical higher-level abstractions and an event loop into the mix, whereas this pure PHP example is as bare bones as it gets, so they are not completely interchangeable examples.

Add Some Logging

As fantastic as it is to get a response from our HTTP server in a web browser, it would be nice if we could also log each and every request for the purposes of debugging. The trouble is we have a nice pure function used to handle the response to an HTTP request, and we do not want to place another concern (logging) into such a tidy function. We can make use of a closure to combine the calls to our functions.

First up is the logging function, which just writes the request method (GET, POST, etc.) and the request path (/, /page-name) to a log file called access_log.

```php
$lh = function($request) {
    $fh = fopen('access_log', 'a');
    fwrite($fh,
        "{$request->getMethod()}: {$request->getPath()}\n");
    fclose($fh);
};
```

We can also make a minor change to the definition of the request handler ($rh) so it only takes the one parameter ($response) it actually needs:

```php
$rh = function($response) {
    $response->writeHead(200, [
        'Content-Type' => 'text/plain'
    ]);
    $response->end("Sakubona, unjani?");
};
```

To map the functions, we will wrap them up in a handy closure so they can be called subsequently to each other:

```php
$eh = function($request, $response) use($rh, $lh) {
    $rh($response);
    $lh($request);
};
```

Finally, update the request handler binding line to match:

```php
$http->on('request', $eh);
```

If you now execute this code by visiting http://127.0.0.1:7355 in your browser, you will be presented with the same message, but your log file will contain something like:

```
GET: /
GET: /favicon.ico
```

The second request is the web browser being hopeful and trying to find a favicon on our server. Of course, there isn't one on our server, but without logging, we would never have known the server was being hit twice on each request.

Introduce a Monad

So far, we have set up a simple web server with a small amount of functional code. Next up, we have an urgent demand for our server to process user requests. Now of course, the following code is not really written with production in mind and serves more as a jumping off point and example of monad usage.

Since you have already seen the Maybe monad, we will take that idea and extend it a little bit by combining it with a list monad. This will provide predictable access to the GET parameters which are passed in the request to our little ReactPHP web server. For the sake of transparency, this monad will be named QueryList. As you may predict, it will be a container for the query string array.

Like the last container monad, we must extend Monad, define the basic constructor and class property to act as our container. Also in this case, the pack() function is very simple as it accepts an array and returns the same array wrapped up in a new QueryList container—the default monadic behavior of Monad.

Listing 8.1
```
01. class QueryList extends Monad
02. {
03.     public function flatMap(callable $f) {
04.         return static::pack(array_map($f, $this->container));
05.     }
06.
07.     public function isNothing($index = null) {
08.         return (null === $index) ?
09.             !(count($this->container)) :
10.             !(array_key_exists($index, $this->container));
11.     }
12.
13.     public function get($index = null) {
14.         return (null === $index) ?
15.             $this->container :
16.             $this->container[$index];
17.     }
18.
19.     public function getOrElse($index = null, $default = []) {
20.         return ($this->isNothing($index)) ?
21.             $default :
22.             $this->get($index);
23.     }
24. }
```

Again, the map() method is really quite simple in the case of this monad, but we have created a new flatMap() method to augments its functionality. It takes the contained array and simply uses array_map() to apply a function to each value in the array before returning the resulting array wrapped up into a new instance of QueryList.

With the basic monad functions out of the way, it is time to discuss the problem-specific methods. The first of these is the isNothing() method, which we saw in the Maybe monad. For our QueryList monad, we must make a couple of modifications to facilitate the checks which are required. The code must know if the whole container is empty or—if supplied—if a particular index in the container is nothing.

As you can see, this is done through the use of a ternary to determine if an index has been supplied and a simple, in-place Boolean checks against the existence in/of the container. This method, much like in the Maybe example, will be used later internally, but it can also be useful publicly as well.

To be able to obtain a value from the container, we must add a get method in Listing 8.1, much like in the Maybe monad. There is, of course, one very slight change to handle obtaining a particular index from the contained array if the optional $index parameter is supplied.

To make our access more robust, we will also create a simple little getOrElse() method, which will give us access to an index or the whole array. If the requested aspect of the container isNothing(), then it will return the supplied default value instead. Again, this is of course, a very similar method to the similarly named function in the Maybe monad.

There you have it—a custom monad written for the job at hand. As you know, it is built upon the groundwork in the Maybe monad and has been slightly augmented with list-processing specific functionality. This allows us to easily wrap up the GET query items in a robust container to facilitate easy universal access. Not only that—it also provides a very handy way of applying functions to the internal list. To that end, let us now define a simple lambda to wrap htmlspecialchars().

```
$html_escape = function($string) {
    $flags = ENT_COMPAT;
    if(version_compare(PHP_VERSION, '5.4.0', '>=')) {
        $flags |= ENT_HTML5;
    }
    return htmlspecialchars($string, $flags, 'UTF-8');
};
```

In order to support UTF-8 in PHP 5.3 and still set the correct document type flag for PHP 5.4, we must have some simple version checking logic. This means we have ended up with a very basic wrapping function we can now apply/map against our QueryList monad.

Before we can do that, however, we must define the ReactPHP server which will supply its GET parameters to us. Just like last time, we need to implement an event handler with:

```
$eh = function($request, $response) use ($html_escape) {
    $ql = QueryList::pack($request->getQuery());
    $ql = $ql->map($html_escape);
    $response->writeHead(200, array(
        'Content-Type' => 'text/html'
    ));
    $response->end($ql->getOrElse('foo', 'A default value'));
};
```

At the moment, this takes in the request, extracts the query parameters, and packs them into a QueryList monad. We then map $html_escape() to each value in the array, which goes through applying htmlspecialchars(). The code then plucks one particular index and prints it as the response.

Of course, none of this will run until we set up ReactPHP's event loop and bind the event handler $eh().

```
$loop = React\EventLoop\Factory::create();
$socket = new React\Socket\Server($loop);
$http = new React\Http\Server($socket, $loop);

$http->on('request', $eh);
$socket->listen(7355);
$loop->run();
```

With that complete you can start the server on the command line as before and visit http://127.0.0.1:7355?foo=bar to see bar printed to your web page. To see the $html_escape() lambda in action, we will need to pass in some URL-encoded special characters instead of bar:

http://127.0.0.1:7355?foo=%3Cbang%3E

This will print the result (<bang>) to screen in a properly HTML-encoded manner.

Now you have seen some event-driven programming and employed a monad to save yourself from painful list interactions, but what is this hiding around the corner? Callback hell! If you have ever written in an event-driven way before, you have probably encountered the issue of having deeply-nested callback functions rendering illegible code. There are a few patterns we can use to avoid this issue which will be covered in the next section.

Callback Wrangling

Event-driven programming, if left to its own devices, can quickly enter a stage known as *callback hell*. Unfortunately, the next level is certain death or a major refactor, as the following highly-contrived code exemplifies.

Listing 8.2
```
01. function a($v, $cb) { return $cb($v) . 'a'; }
02.
03. function b($v, $cb) { return $cb($v) . 'b'; }
04.
05. function c($v, $cb) { return $cb($v) . 'c'; }
06.
07. function d($v, $cb) { return $cb($v) . 'd'; }
08.
09. $res = a('ndlovu', function($v) {
10.     return b(ucwords($v), function($v) {
11.         return c(strrev($v), function($v) {
12.             return d(str_repeat($v, 3), function($v) {
13.                 return $v;
14.             });
15.         });
16.     });
17. });
18. echo $res; // uvoldNuvoldNuvoldNdcba
```

You can save yourself from this right from the start by adopting some predefined patterns in the code you are producing. To make this deal sweeter, there are some simple, but powerful libraries which make it easier to implement these patterns. This allows you to concentrate on your code, abstracting the problem away.

We're going to review two such libraries with different approaches to the problem. They are both part of the greater ReactPHP project although they are emulations of two different JavaScript libraries.

Async

Starting with the simpler of the two libraries, Async, which is a PHP implementation of the ideas in async.js. It simplifies callbacks by allowing you to define them as lists rather than being nested within each other. Much as before, installation is relatively simple when using Composer in the same directory you experimented with the ReactPHP web server earlier:

```
composer require react/async:~1.0
```

You can either call the functions in parallel or as a waterfall. By using the parallel implementation, you are effectively passing the same call to a set of functions and combining their results in the order they are returned, rather than the order they are defined. This is demonstrated clearly in this example (Listing 8.3) from the project's documentation.

Listing 8.3

```
01. use React\Async\Util as Async;
02.
03. $loop = React\EventLoop\Factory::create();
04. Async::parallel(
05.     array(
06.         function ($callback, $errback) use ($loop) {
07.             $loop->addTimer(1, function () use ($callback) {
08.                 $callback('Slept for a whole second');
09.             });
10.         },
11.         function ($callback, $errback) use ($loop) {
12.             $loop->addTimer(1, function () use ($callback) {
13.                 $callback('Slept for another whole second');
14.             });
15.         },
16.         function ($callback, $errback) use ($loop) {
17.             $loop->addTimer(1, function () use ($callback) {
18.                 $callback('Slept for yet another whole second');
19.             });
20.         },
21.     ),
22.     function (array $results) {
23.         foreach ($results as $result) {
24.             var_dump($result);
25.         }
26.     },
27.     function (\Exception $e) {
28.         throw $e;
29.     }
30. );
31. $loop->run();
32. // string(24) "Slept for a whole second"
33. // string(34) "Slept for yet another whole second"
34. // string(30) "Slept for another whole second"
```

The waterfall model is different because it will pass the return value from the preceding function as a parameter into the next one. In this way, the functions return their results in the order they were defined. Listing 8.4 is again taken from the documentation of the React/Async project.

Listing 8.4

```
01. use React\Async\Util as Async;
02.
03. $loop = React\EventLoop\Factory::create();
04. $addOne = function ($prev, $callback = null) use ($loop) {
05.     if (!$callback) {
06.         $callback = $prev;
07.         $prev = 0;
08.     }
09.     $loop->addTimer(1, function () use ($prev, $callback) {
10.         $callback($prev + 1);
11.     });
12. };
13. Async::waterfall(array(
14.     $addOne,
15.     $addOne,
16.     $addOne,
17.     function ($prev, $callback) use ($loop) {
18.         echo "Final result is $prev\n";
19.         $callback();
20.     },
21. ));
22. $loop->run();
23. // Final result is 3
```

Here you have two simple methods for reigning in wild callback functions, but I promised more! The next library is an implementation of a subset of the functionality found in CommonJS.

Promises

This pattern is known as a promise, and it is a little more complex, and more powerful to boot. A piece of code can make a promise to return a certain value once its asynchronous operation (known as a deferred) is complete. We do not want to delay execution, so we take it at its word and accept a placeholder instead. This placeholder, or promise, can be passed from function to function until the result is required to continue execution. In the case of a database write, you can stick it into an asynchronous operation and watch for a result to display a notification or attempt a retry of the save.

React/Promise also makes it possible to manage the processing of many operations. We will only address a small subset of its functionality here, although there is more documentation on the GitHub page for the project[2]. The contrived example which follows would actually be broken out through the layers of your application so it is more for illustrative purposes.

First, we need to install React/Promise using Composer, and the installation instructions remain the same as specified previously.

```
composer require react/promise:~1.0
```

[2]   React/Promise: https://github.com/reactphp/promise

To begin with, we will create a simple logging function called elog(), which is short for *echo log*. It will take a title, a body, and an option to print or return the formatted log.

```php
function elog($title, $body = '', $return = false) {
    $body = (empty($body)) ?: ": {$body}" . PHP_EOL;
    $log = PHP_EOL . "{$title}{$body}";
    if ($return) {
        return $log;
    }
    echo $log;
}
```

Next up is a simple PHP function object which will handle reading a stream from the Unix random source at /dev/urandom. For the sake of being obvious, we will call this class ReadStream.

```php
class ReadStream {
    protected $resolver = null;
    protected $data = null;
}
```

> /dev/urandom *is a non-blocking source of random binary information on POSIX systems. It is similar in nature to* /dev/random, *but it is cryptographically less secure as it reuses the internal entropy pool to generate pseudo-random bits. This reuse makes it potentially less secure, but for our purposes, it will do nicely.*
>
> *If you are following along on a Windows machine, then there is no simple equivalent of* /dev/random—*or for that matter,* /dev/urandom—*so you can simply use a large text file as your source for the following examples.*

You have a simple class with two properties for later use, so let's add a static method to bind a resolver (a tracking component of the promise library) and return a new instance of ReadStream.

```php
public static function bind($resolver) {
    $that = new static;
    $that->setResolver($resolver);
    return $that;
}
```

The resolver is set using a class method as you saw in the previous code block, so let's define it:

```php
public function setResolver($resolver) {
    $this->resolver = $resolver;
}
```

The final method to be added to the ReadStream function object is the magic __invoke() function.

```php
public function __invoke($stream, $loop) {
    $rand = base64_encode(fread($stream, 16));
    $this->data .= $rand;
    $this->resolver->progress($rand);
    if (strlen($this->data) > 1000) {
        $this->resolver->resolve($this->data);
    }
}
```

To break down its operation, we will begin with the first line of the function. It reads 16 bytes from the file stream and then encodes them using base 64. This gives us a string representation of the binary data which is read from the random source.

This is then added to the `data` class property so we can maintain some state between asynchronous calls to this function object. As each line of random is processed, the code calls `progress()` on the promise to log the status of the asynchronous code. Finally, if we have more than one thousand characters of random information, we mark the promise as fulfilled.

To get the random stream first, we must get a file resource handle and set it as a non-blocking stream.

```
$fh = fopen('/dev/urandom', 'rb');
stream_set_blocking($fh, 0);
```

So far, the code has barely even touched upon the functionality React/Promise makes available, but this is about to change! It all begins with the declaration of a new deferred promise and a set of callbacks to handle results from the promise's resolver.

Listing 8.5
```
01. $deferred = new React\Promise\Deferred;
02. $deferred->promise()->then(
03.     function ($result) {
04.         return $result;
05.     }, // 1
06.     function ($reason) {
07.         elog('Rejected', $reason);
08.     }, // 2
09.     function ($update) {
10.         elog('Update', $update);
11.     } // 3
12. )->then(
13.     function($str) {
14.         return elog('Random', $str, true);
15.     }
16. )->then(
17.     function($str) {
18.         echo $str;
19.     }
20. );
```

The `then()` methods are called in sequence when the promise relays an event such as its progress being updated or it finally being resolved. Let's focus on the latter for now as we see the result returned from the first `then()` block is passed as the input to the second.

Looking at the first `then()` block, you can see it accepts three callback functions. The first is called when the promise is successfully resolved. When a promise fails to be resolved, the second function will be called. Progress updates will trigger the third and final callback function. Returning a value from any of these functions will cause it to be supplied as the input parameter to the respective function in the next `then()` block.

As you can see in the subsequent `then()` block, the callbacks are optional. The second and third `then()` blocks are defined with only the successful callbacks supplied. The workings of these callback functions are so simplistic I am not going to go into any further detail.

To put this into action, we will need a simple event loop, and as before, React/event-loop fills this need admirably.

```
$loop = React\EventLoop\Factory::create();
$loop->addReadStream($fh,
   ReadStream::bind($deferred->resolver())
);
$loop->run();
```

This creates a new event loop, adds a read stream to it by binding the promise to the file handle, and finally, the loop is run. When executed, the code we have laid out will print a list of updates (in real time) followed by a printout of all the results combined into one long result string.

This is a nice introduction to promises, but it would be remiss of me to skip over the more powerful combinatory functionality React/Promise also provides. To allow me to cover the reduce operation, we will need to define another deferred promise before the event loop.

First, though, we must open a new file resource handle and set it to be a non-blocking stream.

```
$fh2 = fopen('/dev/urandom', 'rb');
stream_set_blocking($fh2, 0);
```

The second deferred is essentially the same as the first, but with references changed to include '2nd'.

Listing 8.6

```
01. $second_deferred = new React\Promise\Deferred;
02. $second_deferred->promise()->then(
03.     function ($result) {
04.         return $result;
05.     },
06.     function ($reason) {
07.         elog('2nd Rejected', $reason);
08.     },
09.     function ($update) {
10.         elog('2nd Update', $update);
11.     }
12. )->then(
13.     function($str) {
14.         return elog('2nd Random', $str, true);
15.     }
16. )->then(
17.     function($str) {
18.         echo $str;
19.     }
20. );
```

To combine the two promises, we will use a reduce operation by implementing When::reduce(), which takes an array of the deferred as its first parameter. The second parameter is a callback function that performs the combination logic and returns a new deferred promise wrapping the result.

You can then apply then() function blocks to this deferred to gain access to the final result.

Listing 8.7

```
01. React\Promise\When::reduce(
02.    array($deferred, $second_deferred),
03.    function($ignored, $value) {
04.       static $temp = '';
05.       return $temp = $temp . $value;
06.    }
07. )->then(
08.    function($result) {
09.       elog('Final', $result);
10.       return $result;
11.    }
12. )->then(
13.    function($result) {
14.       elog('Final MD5', md5($result));
15.    }
16. );
```

The first then() block simply elog()'s the result of the combination and also returns the result for use in the next then() block. The final then() block prints out an MD5 hash of the result from the reduce operation.

To execute this code, you will need to bind it to the deferred in the event loop again, like:

```
$loop = React\EventLoop\Factory::create();
$loop->addReadStream($fh,
   ReadStream::bind($deferred->resolver())
);
$loop->addReadStream($fh2,
   ReadStream::bind($second_deferred->resolver())
);
$loop->run();
```

When this code is run, you will get a debug log for each read from both the first and second deferred. Each deferred will then print its result.

Finally, the When::reduce() will print a combination of both the first and second deferred along with an MD5 hash of the result. There are a number of other operations you can perform on lists of deferred promises, and these include: map(), some(), any(), all(), and more. Each allow you to make different decisions based upon the results from your deferred promise. Although interesting, it is beyond our scope here to go into further detail, but you can easily use the reduce() example as a base to explore the rest of the features of this library. For more information, please see the project's documentation on GitHub[3].

Promises are a very handy way to organize callback functions and prevent them from getting out of control. There are some handy pieces of code to make it easier to handle asynchronous operations in PHP code. PHP is not known for being event-driven, or for asynchronous operations for that matter. Most standard library calls do not run this way—leaving the parser to process the job until it is finished in series. With the help of some libraries, it is possible to bring this power to PHP in an elegant way.

Promises provide one way of helping to mitigate the callback hell that event-driven programming can bring with it.

[3]   React/Promise: https://github.com/reactphp/promise

Wrap Up the Show

Event-driven programming is not only possible in PHP, but thanks to the reactor pattern and ReactPHP, it is easy. While event-driven programming can lead to callback hell, as we have seen, there are a number of libraries and patterns you can adopt to avoid this. Much like functional programming, a lot of the event-driven programming we have reviewed here is experimental. It is fun to play with, but rarely finds itself in production.

There are at least two far more popular alternatives in Node.js (ReactPHP was formerly known as NodePHP) and Python's Twisted. Both of these have seen far more time in production than PHP's event libraries. This can be attributed to PHP's focus on short-running processes for a web server. Sure, it can be run as a daemon with libraries like PHPDaemon[4] and PHP Simple Daemon[5], but the supporting tooling, however, is not as mature as the competition.

All of this combines to make it a really small niche in PHP programming, but as Igor Wiedler (React-PHP's creator) says: "anything they can have, we can steal!"

[4] PHPDaemon: http://daemon.io
[5] PHP Simple Daemon: http://github.com/shaneharter/PHP-Daemon

Chapter 9

Hazards of Functional Programming in PHP

"'I am not going to exploit functional programming because my coworkers would complain' is such a gross and cynical thing to believe."

–Tony Morris (Functional programmer, _@dibblego_)

PHP is not a functional language, and therefore, it is more than a lack of syntactic sugar we must overcome. Or more likely in PHP's case, work around and make do! As a language, PHP has not evolved to support the use of functions as we need, and there has been a deliberate choice to concentrate development resources on improving the language's object-oriented capabilities. I am not criticizing this; given limited resources, it is important you focus on aspects which will have the greatest impact. Catering to a minority of PHP developers while ignoring the masses would hamper continued uptake of the language and disenfranchise current users.

Having said all this, it is of course, frustrating when a language you are using is not able to cater to the code you wish to implement with it. "Use a more appropriate language," you might quite rightly cry! I would counter there are a great number of developers who are immensely productive in PHP and may wish to use those skills in a functional style. More practically, there are those of us who must use PHP for various reasons such as it is the only deployment platform, integration with a legacy codebase, or it is an employer's mandate.

All of this means you will need to think about how you are going to manage your functional projects in PHP. First, how will you lay out your files and create functional "packages" for code sharing?

Unfortunately, PHP does not have a mechanism for autoloading functions at present and from following the discussions surrounding two related PHP RFCs[1], it would appear the feature is never coming or, at least, is a very long way off.

Which leaves you with a few choices:

1. Require/include in all the files for all requests.
2. Set up the functions as static methods in a class file, which can then be autoloaded similar to Underscore.php[2].
3. Use my simple functions which cause namespace use statements to perform more like an import clause. While it solves a problem, it is—at its core—a complete hack which will invariably slow down your code due to the use of the PHP Tokenizer to double parse the files[3].

This is not a show stopper, but it's annoying and does merit mentioning. If you are going to be implementing some basic functional styles, then it does not matter so much, but if you want to share or reuse a whole library of functions, then you are faced with these three horrible options.

Additional caveats include not being able to simply import one function from a namespace or alias which function in your use statement. You could potentially work around the former by putting each function into its own namespace. You could then use the narrower namespace to pull in just the one function.

There is a miserable trade-off, though, as it will make calling the function a more verbose procedure. If you import the parent namespace, for instance, you would need to specify the child namespace before each function call:

```
use Treffynnon as T;

T\Sort\sort($collection, $callable_function);
```

However, it would allow you to pull in just one function like so:

```
use Treffynnon\Sort as TS;

TS\sort($collection, $callable_function);
```

Handling immutable data is complicated by the fact PHP does not support it natively, and it is the functional developer's responsibility to ensure they do not introduce state changes into the code themselves. There have been a few attempts to enforce immutable data in PHP, but none of them are particularly satisfactory and all of them require class-based trickery such as Mikko Koppanen's php-immutable extension[4]—a self-described hack.

You are now in the uncharted wilds of PHP and pushing the boundaries of what is possible all the time. Things will be sub-optimal at times or just down right impossible, so you will need to use your judgement as to when these techniques are best employed—if at all—in your projects.

Another minor issue is other PHP developers may struggle to understand your code and curse your name!

---

[1] Autofunc RFC: https://wiki.php.net/rfc/autofunc
     and Function Loading RFC: https://wiki.php.net/rfc/function_autoloading
[2] Underscore.php: http://brianhaveri.github.com/Underscore.php/
[3] Namespace Importer: https://github.com/treffynnon/namespace-importer
[4] php-immutable extension: https://github.com/mkoppanen/php-immutable

Chapter

10

Advances in PHP

(*"When there's a will to fail, obstacles can be found."*

— John McCarthy
(Computer scientist and LISP programming language,
1927–2011))

PHP 5.4

With the introduction of PHP 5.4, a few new features have been added which make programming in a functional style easier.

Callables

The first of these additions is the callable type hint[1] that can be applied to a function's parameters, thereby ensuring the passed value is a callback. The specification of the callback can be a string containing the name of a PHP function, a lambda function or closure, array class notation, or a static method as a string representation.

[1] *Callable Type: http://php.net/language.types.callable*

```
$seed_data = array('BIZA', 'IBIZO', 'LAMI');
function callable_func($collection, callable $callback) {
    return array_map($callback, $collection);
}
$result  = callable_func($seed_data, 'strtolower');
$result2 = callable_func($seed_data, function($value) {
    return ucwords(strtolower($value));
});
```

Short Array Syntax

Next up is a handy addition to make defining arrays a little easier on the keyboard, which has been snappily named: short array syntax, and it works like this:

```
$seed_data = [ 'BIZA', 'IBIZO', 'LAMI' ];
$key_data  = [
    'call' => 'BIZA',
    'name' => 'IBIZO',
    'mine' => 'LAMI'
];
```

Array Dereferencing

Isn't it annoying when you can't skip straight to a certain array element returned from a function call? With array dereferencing now in the PHP core, a pet peeve of mine—for as long as I can remember—has now been fixed.

```
function get_map() {
    return [ 'version' => '1.2.4', 'build' => '20151012' ];
}
echo get_map()['build']; // 20151012
```

In a similar vein, you can now also access class members on instantiation—although unfortunately, it is not possible to call functors in this way.

```
(new Foo)->bar(); // calls the bar() method successfully
// (new SumFunctor)(5, 10); // throws a parse error :(

// the closest you can get is:
(new SumFunctor)->__invoke(5, 10);
```

This bug was fixed as an oversight in PHP 7[2].

There is one further implementation detail supported by closures in PHP 5.4 which, while not strictly applicable to functional programming, deserves a quick mention. You can bind a class to a closure instance to make the class available as $this within the closure. This saves you from having to pass in the context via a use statement incorporating the $this—$that dance.

PHP 5.5

With 5.5 there is a new list of features available. Here are my picks for functional programming.

Generators

Generators are simple constructs which allow you to bring the lazy loading style functionality to building arrays such as those returned by range().

[2]   class member access using __invoke() in php5.4: https://bugs.php.net/bug.php?id=63253

Instead of building the whole array in one hit up front, it will generate the next item just in time for the next iteration, which results in significant memory savings. Here is an example taken from the PHP manual:

```
function xrange($start, $limit, $step = 1) {
    for ($i = $start; $i <= $limit; $i += $step) {
        yield $i;
    }
}
echo F\sum(xrange(1, 10)); // 55
```

Empty() and Functional Values

The `empty()` language construct can now take function return values directly:

```
function another_function() {
    return empty(some_function());
}
```

Other Additions

It will now also be possible to dereference arrays and string literals directly:

```
echo [ 1, 2, 3, 4, 5 ][2]; // 3
echo 'ikhanda'[4]; // n
```

As previously mentioned, PHP will also receive array pluck functionality in the form of the `array_column()` function.

PHP 5.6

Variadics

Nikita proposed an RFC which defines syntax for variadic functions in PHP 5.6[3]. This is a handy feature which adds a symbol to a function that can take unlimited arguments and replaces the annoyances required when using the current `func_get_args()` method.

```
function prln($title) {
    $messages = array_slice(func_get_args(), 1);
    echo "$title: " . implode(', ', $messages);
}
```

This becomes the far simpler and more obvious:

```
function prln($title, ...$messages) {
    echo "$title: " . implode(', ', $messages);
}
```

The feature has now shipped with PHP 5.6 and is available to be used in production now.

[3] Variadics RFC: *https://wiki.php.net/rfc/variadic*

List Type Checking

With the addition of variadics to the language it is now possible to check type hint the contents of an array in a very naive way on functions. It works for a one dimensional array of PHP objects to ensure each value in the array is of a certain type and that is all. To make this work, we will use the variadic and splat operator to expand the array into function arguments and then assemble it back into an array again.

```
function set_dates(DateTimeInterface ...$dates) {
    return $dates;
}
```

The code above can be applied to a list of objects as the example below shows.

```
$ds = [new DateTime(), new DateTime];
set_dates(...$ds);
// [DateTime, DateTime]
```

The call to **set_dates()** using the array of objects with the . . . keyword is functionally equivalent to:

```
set_dates(new DateTime(), new DateTime());
// [DateTime, DateTime]
```

An incorrect type being passed into the function will trigger a catchable error as demonstrated here:

```
$ds = [new DateTime(), 0];
set_dates(...$ds);
// TypeError: Argument 2 passed to set_dates() must implement
//            interface DateTimeInterface, integer given
```

Namespaces

With PHP 5.6 namespacing functions got a little easier with the ability to import a specific function instead of the entire namespace in the example above. Note the function keyword included in the use statement to indicate we are importing a function.

```
namespace Treffynnon\MyExample {
    function e() {
        echo 'A pointless function.';
    }
}

namespace {
    use function Treffynnon\MyExample\e;
    e();
}
```

A particularly handy aspect of this development is it's now possible to alias function identifiers when they are imported into a namespace.

```
namespace {
    use function Treffynnon\MyExample\e as p;
    p();
}
```

You can see here the function identifier is aliased at the point it is imported into the namespace with the as keyword. This essentially tells PHP to treat and call to p() as though it is a call directly to e().

For the sake of completeness it is worth pointing out here the same enhancement brought with it the ability to import namespaced constants as well:

```
namespace Treffynnon\MyExample {
    const HARK = 'Some exciting value';
}

namespace {
    use const Treffynnon\MyExample\HARK;
    echo HARK;
}
```

Namespaces are a great way of keeping functions in distinct libraries to prevent naming collisions and maintain logical separations. Additionally, it is now possible to alias a function identifier as it is imported to further assist in avoiding namespace collisions. Tragically it became evident PHP still does not support autoloading of functions and it looks unlikely to do so in the near future.

PHP 7

Following the vote to skip the version number 6 of PHP, it was decided to call PHPNG (next generation) PHP 7. There was once a PHP 6, but it never saw the light of day and remained unmerged into the master PHP branch. It was cancelled for several reasons and some features were backported into the PHP 5.x branch. Before it got cancelled, though, a number of companies wrote books, articles, and blog posts about it. These are still accessible via your favorite search engine!

The PHP team decided it would be too confusing to call what is now being released PHP 6, All those old resources would come up and they would be inaccurate. So the version number was consigned to history.

A number of new features have been added to the language alongside some bug fixes and speed enhancements. A lot of effort has been put in by many members of the PHP language team. This has resulted in PHP's greatest release yet. There are a few new features I will highlight here which can be useful while producing functional PHP code. It goes without saying there are plenty of other features and improvements to the language so if I have missed your favorite I apologize. Profusely.

Scalar Type Hinting

As of PHP 7 a new RFC was merged into the core of the language to offer scalar type hinting. This is a big step in the right direction for the language so it was fantastic news when it survived the RFC voting process overcoming significant opposition. PHP developers have been waiting for such a feature to arrive for many years and despite previous attempts, it has never made it into the language before.

This new feature set covers the types `int`, `float`, `string` and `bool` allowing them to be used in the same way as we have seen classes, interfaces, `array`, and `callable` used already. A half implemented core language feature has finally moved towards completion.

In addition to these type hints it is also possible to indicate that you want strict type checking. If activated, the parser will throw an `E_RECOVERABLE_ERROR` when incorrect types are passed in as parameters to the function. As you would expect I recommend you always develop with strict types enabled to assist you in a creating more robust code. It can be activated by simply including the following at the top of your file:

```
declare(strict_types=1);
```

All function calls in that file will now be treated in a strict manner.

By default, all PHP files are parsed in weak typed checking mode so you will have to declare this atop every file. Perhaps a macro in your IDE on new file creation to automatically add this declaration would keep you from forgetting to add this vital ingredient.

With the declaration in place the PHP parser will help you maintain your code by alerting you to type mismatches and violations. This flies in the face of PHP's traditional approach of automatically coalescing all values to the correct type where possible. While this does take a "run at all costs" approach, it means poorly written code will still work allowing simple bugs to go undetected.

A function may be declared with type hints against its parameters to cause the PHP parser to check the type of the value passed to the function. In strict mode, an error will be thrown if the types do not match. In the more permissive mode, the PHP engine will cast the arguments to the desired types. In previous versions of PHP you would have had to do this yourself using `gettype` or similar.

```php
function sum(array $vals, int $start) {
    return array_sum($vals) + $start;
}
$a = sum([1, 2, 3], 10); // 16
// $b = sum([1, 2, 3], 'ibizo'); // E_RECOVERABLE_ERROR
```

It is trivially easy to accidentally reverse the parameters of a function when calling it, so this simple parser error checking helps to catch it. Obviously if both parameters are of the same type then this will not help you! You can see the sort of bug this will help you to avoid though.

Return Type Declarations

Also in PHP 7 another RFC was merged called return type declarations, which compliments the scalar type hints RFC excellently. It allows you to declare the type that should be returned from a function. The parser does not require a type to be defined on a function return value, but much like the strict declaration in scalar type hints I would suggest it is good practice to do so.

To specify a return type you simply add a colon after the closing parenthesis of the function and then include the expected type keyword such as `int` or `array`.

You can also declare classes or interfaces you have written yourself as return types much like you can with function arguments.

```php
class MyClass {}

function get_class_inst(): MyClass {
    return new MyClass;
}
```

It is not currently possible to have multiple return types for a function. This means you cannot say, return an `int` on success or `null` on failure for example—it must be one or the other. Again, much like with the scalar type hints if there is a type mismatch then an `E_RECOVERABLE_ERROR` will be triggered.

This brings more powerful type checking to PHP along with a reduction in bugs. It also makes the code easier to reason about and assemble in your mind when you come back to it. Finally, IDE's and other tools can be smarter when inspecting the code you write.

Where possible, ensure you declare strict mode for type hints and make sure you include a return type declaration. This will help to make sure you enjoy the benefits of these PHP 7 features. There are some limitations too, but if you are writing good code then you shouldn't run into them. Use it for its strengths and you will be a happier developer than yesterday.

In Listing 10.1 I have included a few examples of how this can be used to great effect.

Listing 10.1

```
01. function sum(array $arr, callable $func): int {
02.     return array_reduce($arr, $func, 0);
03. }
04.
05. $a = sum([1, 2, 3, 4], function(int $c, int $v) {
06.     return $c + $v;
07. }); // 10
08.
09. $b = sum([1, '10', 'twenty'], function(string $c, string $v) {
10.     return $c . $v;
11. }); // E_RECOVERABLE_ERROR as return type must be int, but here a string is supplied.
12.
13. class MyInt {
14.     private $int = 0;
15.     public function __construct(int $v) {
16.         $this->int = $v;
17.     }
18.     public function get(): int {
19.         return $this->int;
20.     }
21.     public function getHuman(): string {
22.         // user intl extension to PHP
23.         $nf = new \NumberFormatter('en_us', \NumberFormatter::SPELLOUT);
24.         return $nf->format($this->int);
25.     }
26. }
27.
28. $ten = new MyInt(10); // Int(10)
29. $word = $ten->getHuman(); // string('ten')
30. $int = $ten->get(); // int(10)
31.
32. // $eleven = new MyInt('eleven'); // E_RECOVERABLE_ERROR
```

Some of the silly errors caught by the parser in Listing 10.1 are easy to miss and cause programs to malfunction unexpectedly. Enabling type hinting and adding return type declarations can help to ensure this does not happen.

As mentioned previously there are a host of other improvements to the language and the Zend runtime itself. These include new features and, frankly amazing performance enhancements. There are so many reasons to upgrade; hopefully it will be deployed to PAAS and hosts around the world quickly as this is, of course, the best release yet.

Namespace Group Syntax

With PHP 7 the namespace syntax has been expanded to include group use statements that greatly reduce the amount of typing required. It comes into play when you want to specify multiple namespaces you want to use from the same parent namespace.

To make this simpler let us assume we have a namespace `\Treffynnon\FunctionalPhp` and underneath that the following classes:

1. `Html`
2. `Date`
3. `Blog`
4. `ShoppingList`

Rendering a blog post requires the first, second, and third classes, but not the last. We would use group statements to pull in just those items we want:

```
use \Treffynnon\FunctionalPhp\{ Html, Date, Blog };
```

While this feature will inevitably have limited use it is handy to know of and could save you some effort when dealing with PHP's clumsy namespace syntax.

Closure Calls

In PHP 7 closure behavior in the language has been augmented with bind at call time execution. As mentioned earlier PHP 5 has the `bind` and `bindTo` methods, but they must be called before execution. This can create unnecessary lines of code the new `call` method dispenses with in favor of binding the closure to the class at call time.

```
$c = new stdClass;
$c->value = 10;
$c_instance = function($v) {
  return $v + $this->value;
};
$sum = $c_instance->call($c, 10); // int(20)
```

The previous example provides a neater and simpler method of calling closures in a bound state.

Further into the Future

While it is difficult to tell what will be accepted into future versions of PHP beyond that of the RFCs which have completed votes against them, there has been some discussion on the PHP internals list[4] of adding list comprehension functions. It would be quite a boon for PHP were these features to be added to the language so I will cover them here in the hope that greater awareness leads to greater demand!

Nikita Popov has provided a patch[5] which uses the following syntax to describe a list comprehension.

```
// get a list of registration numbers
$registration_numbers = [foreach ($service_logs as $log)
  yield $log['rego']
];

// this is equivalent to the following code
$registration_numbers = array();
foreach($service_logs as $log) {
  $registration_numbers[] = $log['rego'];
}
```

It would also be possible to filter records to return only records which have the registration number of

[4] [PHP-DEV] *List comprehensions and generator expressions for PHP:*
     http://markmail.org/thread/uvendztpe2rrwiif
[5] *addListComprehensions Branch: https://github.com/nikic/php-src/tree/addListComprehensions*

DG44-001:

```
$filtered_records =
  [foreach ($service_logs as $log) if ($log == 'DG44-001')
    yield $log
  ];
```

The final advantage is the ability for the system to work on nested foreach statements like so (example taken directly from Nikita's introductory email) reproduced in Listing 10.2.

Listing 10.2
```
01. $a_list = array('A', 'B');
02. $b_list = array(1, 2);
03. $combinations = [foreach ($a_list as $a)
04.       foreach ($b_list as $b)
05.       yield array($a, $b)
06.    ];
07.
08. // array(
09. //    array('A', 1),
10. //    array('A', 2),
11. //    array('B', 1),
12. //    array('B', 2)
13. // )
```

As you can see, this is a powerful feature that would make operating on arrays in PHP far easier, and given their succinct nature coupled with a stateless operation, they would make a good addition to the functional programming toolkit.

As PHP moves into the future, it looks like the new versions will add more features and functions which should help to make functional programming a solid reality in PHP.

Chapter

11

Conclusion

"Functional programming is 'just another tool' in the sense that being honest is a technique in addition to just making things up."

—Rúnar Bjarnason (Functional programmer, *@runarorama*)

This book has introduced you to some functional programming techniques you can use in your PHP projects today. While this serves as a good primer in a language you know, I would suggest if you wish to take things further, you should begin looking at other languages such as Haskell, Scala, or Clojure. I find it easier to learn new concepts in a language I am very familiar with, so this has been directed at similar individuals.

In my own projects, I do use some functional methodologies, but those I have released with open source licenses have so far all been written in object-oriented PHP. This reflects the PHP preference for imperative code over functional programming. It is also true of my commercial code, although I hope in the future, these techniques will become more widely understood. We need more functional efforts to be released as open source, more discussions to be had, more speakers to present, and of course, more blog and magazine articles to be written.

That is not to say there are not any open source projects out there making use of functional constructs in their code. A few examples I am aware of are ReactPHP (event-driven framework), Bullet (self-described functional web framework), Slim (micro-framework), and Pimple (dependency injection container)–although none of them (to my knowledge) make use of the more complex functional techniques and generally will include the odd lambda or closure here and there. I am sure there are many other projects also using similar code—if you know of an interesting one I have missed, let me know.

If you wish to get involved in the development of functional programming in PHP, the best places to start are the main PHP internals mailing list and the RFCs[1] on the PHP Wiki[2]. Also functional-php, Underscore.php, and Functionals are all accepting quality pull requests through GitHub.

[1] *Current PHP RFCs: https://wiki.php.net/rfc*
[2] *The PHP.net wiki: https://wiki.php.net*

Appendix

Additional Notes

Understanding Type Signatures

PHP has a weak typing structure so type definitions will most likely be foreign to you. In reality they are pretty simple and in the case of this book simply describe input and output.

When you think of a function in PHP it is common to look at the arguments it accepts. If the function is documented in the PHP manual or completely with something like PHPDoc not only will the arguments be listed, but also their expected return type.

In the case of substr() this is defined as:

```
substr(string $string, int $start [, int $length])
```

To work over the basics of the PHP manual syntax we will start at the beginning of the definition.

1. substr() is the name of the function itself.
2. The next instance of string specifies the type of value which will be passed into the first parameter ($string in the example).
3. $string is the name given to the first argument passed into the function.
4. The comma denotes the end of the $string argument and indicates the presence of another following argument ($start).
5. Next up, we have another type specification (int) for $start.
6. $start is the variable name for the second argument.
7. Then, the opening square bracket indicates an optional parameter coming up.
8. The comma indicates the end of $start and the beginning of the optional parameter $length.
9. $length is the third and optional variable name.

In a nutshell, from the function signature it is possible to deduce the function `substr()` takes two parameters plus one optional parameter. The first parameter should be a string, the second should be an integer, with the third being optional and an integer. The names of the variables do not really matter to us as we are just calling the function and not actually implementing its inner workings.

So that covers input to the function, but what about the equally important return type?

Given the two or three arguments, the expected output is a value of type `string`. I deliberately left this out of the earlier definition for brevity's sake and the complete definition should actually be:

```
string substr(string $string, int $start [, int $length])
```

Note in PHP 7, the syntax for return types requires it to be after the function definition. In this section, we're focusing on how return types have been presented in documentation.

The initial `string` keyword denotes the return type of a function. In other words, this indicates a value of type `string` will be emitted from the `substr()` when it is called.

Often, similar documentation is available via API manuals in userland code. The formats used are often easily compiled into an API manual with a command line utility such as PHPDoc or Doxygen.

These look something like this version of `substr()` for PHPDoc:

```
/**
 * Returns the portion of string specified by the start and length parameters.
 * @param string $string
 * @param int $start
 * @param int $length
 * @return string
 */
```

As you can see this specifies the same details as the PHP manual version, but each parameter is described more verbosely over multiple lines. In PHP 5 that is pretty much it for type definitions—they exist in documentation only, if they exist at all. This trait works out just fine if everyone implementing the function is perfect and passes in the correct arguments, but in my experience this is rarely true.

It is much better to put the definitions into code so the compiler can help you to identify errors easily and quickly. If you wanted to do this prior to PHP 7, then you would have to consider checking the types of the function's arguments with `if` statements. When arguments fail to meet the expected requirements you would throw a fatal error.

Listing A.1

```
01. function substr2($string, $start, $length = null) {
02.     if (!is_string($string)) {
03.         trigger_error('$string must be of type string', E_USER_ERROR);
04.     }
05.
06.     if (!is_int($start)) {
07.         trigger_error('$start must be of type int', E_USER_ERROR);
08.     }
09.
10.     if (!is_null($length) && !is_int($length)) {
11.         trigger_error('$length must be of type int', E_USER_ERROR);
12.     }
13.     return substr($string, $start, $length);
14. }
```

Again, this highlights another important distinction between PHP and more strongly typed languages (functional languages subscribe to the stricter end of this). PHP is a dynamic language, which means the code is parsed at the same time it is run. Any fatal error is going to be triggered when the code executes rather than at compile time and before it is deployed.

Of course, with PHP 7's scalar type and return hints, this function definition becomes much more concise. If the function is called from a file in strict mode, then the engine will throw an error if an argument doesn't match the expected type. In non-strict mode, the PHP engine will cast incoming arguments to the expected type, provided it can do so without data loss.

```php
function substr2(string $string, int $start, int $length = null) :string {
    return substr($string, $start, $length);
}
```

In a compiler based language such as Haskell or Scala it is possible for the contracts (set out with types) to be checked at compiler time rather than at runtime like in PHP. This makes it unlikely you will trigger a type based fatal error when the code is being interacted with. This is why compilers and a strong typing system are very handy.

In PHP you do not have this safety net as incorrect type errors can only be found at runtime. This means that IDEs also cannot reliably hint or show errors based on these type requirements. This has obvious downsides, but on the other hand dynamic languages provide near instant gratification with changes live and executable immediately during development. There are other reasons this is a bad thing, but let us get back to typing.

As we have seen PHP does not enforce types and (sometimes worse) will attempt to coerce values to the correct type for the operation you are attempting. In PHP 5 compatible code, the only scalar type definitions are in comments and therefore unenforceable. In other languages such as Scala or Haskell types are part of the function's definition. Both the parameters and return value of a function are defined using the language's type system. If the incorrect type is returned or passed in, then the compiler will throw an error at build time.

A Scala type definition for the substr() function would look like the following code:

```scala
def substr(string: String, start: Int, length: Int):String = {
    string.substring(start, length)
}
```

This shows a function with the same API as PHP's substr() function, but written in Scala. Well, nearly! To make the code simpler all parameters are required where the PHP function allows the last parameter, $length, to be optional.

Working through it in a similar way to the PHP manual example earlier we come up with a similar list.

1. def is equivalent to PHP's function keyword.
2. substr is the name we are declaring for the function.
3. Next up the function arguments are declared as a comma separated list inside parentheses.
4. The first argument is string which is declared to have the type of String. In Scala the type is declared immediately after the argument name separated by a colon—string: String.
5. start is the name given to our second function argument and it is declared as type Int (accepting an integer). So start: Int means we expect an argument of type Int to be passed into the function. This argument will then be known as start internally to the function.
6. The final argument is length and it has the same definition as start so please see step 5 for a more in depth description.

7. After the parentheses there is another type stated immediately following a colon. In this case it is String because the function will return a string just like the original PHP function this is modeled upon.

The rest of the function definition is just an implementation of the internal workings of substr() which does not warrant further investigation for this book.

There again the same function defined in Haskell is just as descriptive, but written in a slightly different dialect:

```
substr :: String -> Int -> Int -> String
substr string start len =  drop start (take len string)
```

Haskell type definitions are different to those in Scala with their separation from the functions definition being the most stark. The first line is the expected type definition and the second line is the actual implementation.

Looking over the first line it is possible to work through the types as yet another list!

1. First comes the function name substr.

2. Next, two consecutive colons indicate this is a type definition and the definition is coming up next.

3. The type of the first argument is specified first as a String. This is immediately followed by -> which denotes the end of this argument and the presence of another parameter following it. Just like the commas on Scala or PHP (well sort of, but let us not get into that here).

4. As the second argument, this function will take an Int (integer).

5. The third argument is also an Int.

6. The final -> indicates the following type definition will be for the return type of the function. As with the Scala example this is a String.

Again, we will simply skip over the actual implementation as it is not relevant to this book.

The two definitions are simple and their respective languages are capable of being far more expressive. While it might be interesting to dig further into their type systems it is not necessary to understand this book. I have been deliberately liberal in my descriptions of these two type systems to simplify them into the knowledge you need to understand this book. Of course, there is more to both of them, but this is best explored in a Haskell or Scala book.

Throughout the book Haskell syntax will be used to define some types. This is because concepts such as functors, applicatives, and monads are defined within Haskell and are well documented there. This should make it possible for you to review the type signatures of other Haskell monad implementations and build them in PHP too.

If you do decide to explore Haskell or Scala, then it is worth having Hyperpolyglot[1] at hand so you can easily see similar functions across languages.

[1]   Hyperpolyglot: http://hyperpolyglot.org

Using the UTF-8 Ellipsis

During the course of the book a project using three consecutive dots as a function is introduced, the React/Partial[2] library does this. It is a perfectly legal function definition in PHP. The trouble is, it is not just any old set of dots, but one special Unicode character representing an ellipsis. You cannot just hit the dot/full stop/period key on your keyboard three times.

> **CAUTION** *React/Partial uses the Unicode ellipsis character below as a placeholder. It should not be confused with PHP's own . . . syntax for indicating variadic functions[3].*

For smaller usages, the easiest method is to simply copy and paste the character from a UTF-8 table such as *http://www.fileformat.info/info/unicode/char/2026/index.htm*. As you begin to use the function more and more though, it quickly becomes tedious.

If you are lucky enough to be running a version of MacOS then you can simply use a keyboard shortcut. By holding down the Option key and the semi-colon key together you get the character on a QWERTY keyboard. For those on a QWERTZ keyboard it is Option and the period/dot/full stop (.) key. On a Mac the Option key is also known as Alt confusingly.

On Linux there is also a "shortcut", but frankly once you have seen it I am sure you will agree copy and paste looks more appealing. Hold down Ctrl + Shift + u to enter Unicode mode and then 2, 0, 2, 6 and Enter. Some people report Alt Gr and a dot/period/full stop will get an ellipsis out of Linux, but it has never worked properly for me in practice.

Unfortunately, Windows is similarly afflicted as you must press and hold Alt to enter Unicode mode and then press 0, 1, 3, 3 on the number pad releasing the Alt key. If you are on a laptop without a number pad, I'm not sure what you're supposed to do!

If you want an easy copy and paste source you can also make a simple HTML page like *http://www.functionalphp.com/utf8*. The ellipsis character is encoded in HTML as either … and … in HTML.

I tend to use Vim as my text editor of choice and although there is no shortcut by default (why would there be?) it is highly configurable. You can use the imap directive to define a new keymap for use within Vim. In the case of the ellipsis we can define a simple shortcut for Ctrl + F5 –remember you will need to copy and paste the UTF-8 ellipsis character from somewhere to insert into the imap directive.

```
:imap <C-F5> …
```

Now in insert mode within the editor, you can simply hold down the Control and F5 keys at the same time and an ellipsis will be inserted and the point of your cursor. To make this keybinding always available you can add it to your .vimrc with a line:

```
imap <C-F5> …
```

For IDE I am mostly using Netbeans (with Vim keybindings) and much like Vim before it there is no default way of inserting the ellipsis character. You can create a simple macro in the options dialogue that will insert an ellipsis when a keyboard shortcut is pressed.

[2]   React/Partial: *https://github.com/reactphp/partial*
[3]   Variadic Functions: *http://php.net/functions.arguments#functions.variable-arg-list*

You too can enjoy this revelation in four simple steps:

1. Tools > Options > Editor > Macros.
2. Click New and give it a name ("ellipsis" perhaps).
3. Enter the following (include the quotes!) into the Macro Code box: `"…"`.
4. Click Set Shortcut and choose the keystroke you want (I chose `Control + Alt + .`).

Now, by pressing the `Control + Alt + .` keys together a UTF-8 ellipsis character will be inserted into the document at the cursor position.

So the ellipsis is one character and not three dots/periods/full stops in succession. While it may not be simple to use by default there are a few simple techniques to make this easier. While Vim and Netbeans are detailed here I am sure Eclipse, PhpStorm, and Emacs have similar capabilities.

Appendix

B

Resources

"Programmers are the worst people to discuss programming with."

—Brian McKenna (Functional programmer, *@puffnfresh*)

For functional PHP extras and updates, please check out *http://www.functionalphp.com* and follow *@FunctionalPHP* on Twitter.

PHP REPLs

Command line

- phpsh—*http://phpsh.org*
- PsySH—*http://psysh.org*
- Boris—*https://github.com/d11wtq/boris*

Online

- 3v4l—*http://3v4l.org*

Libraries

- functional-php—*https://github.com/lstrojny/functional-php*
- React/Partial—*https://github.com/reactphp/partial*
- nicmart/Functionals—*https://github.com/nicmart/Functionals*
- PHP SuperClosure—*https://github.com/jeremeamia/super_closure*

Other Functional Implementations

- Scala—*http://www.scala-lang.org*
- Haskell—*http://www.haskell.org*
- Idris—*http://www.idris-lang.org*
- Erlang—*http://www.erlang.org*
- Scheme—*http://www.schemers.org*
- Clojure—*http://www.clojure.org*
- Common LISP—*http://common-lisp.net*
- OCaml—*http://ocaml.org*

Online Courses (MOOC)

- Introduction to Functional Programming with Erik Meijer—
  https://www.edx.org/course/introduction-functional-programming-delftx-fp101x-0
- Functional Programming Principles in Scala with Martin Odersky (creator of the Scala programming
  language)—*https://www.coursera.org/course/progfun*
- Principles of Reactive Programming with Martin Odersky, Erik Meijer and Roland Kuhn—
  https://www.coursera.org/course/reactive

Glossary

"The calculus was the first achievement of modern mathematics and it is difficult to overestimate its importance."

—John von Neumann (Mathematician and Physicist, 1903–1957)

??
See *null coalescence*.

?:
See *ternary operator*.

anonymous function
See lambda.

API
Application Programming Interface which can be either external or internally facing.

argument
A value passed to a subroutine. In PHP functions this is passed between the parentheses of the function. Also known interchangeably as a parameter.

```
function x($argument)
```

blocking
A call which halts the progress of the overall application until it completes.

CLI
Command Line Interface which allows usage via a terminal.

closure
An *anonymous function* which can carry context.

collection
Please see *list*.

curly braces
{}

Curry
Both a man (Haskell Curry) and a technique where all function arguments become functions themselves.

deterministic
Processes that are deterministic always return the same result repeatedly.

dot
.

DoxyGen
Generate API documentation from inline code comments.

DSL
Domain Specific Language. Languages designed and built to solve problems in a specific domain such as share trading or fluid dynamics.

Erlang
A functional programming language created in Ericsson Labs.

F#
A functional programming language written on top of the .NET framework.

first class functions
Languages exhibiting the characteristic have functions which can be treated as any other variable allowing them to be passed around by and into other functions.

function
A subroutine which optionally accepts arguments and/or returns a value.

function object
An object which can be called as a function.

functional-php
A PHP library and extension providing functional primitives to PHP.

full stop
.

generator
Language construct allowing for memory efficient processing of lists.

Hack
An extension of the PHP language with its own runtime HHVM.

Haskell
A functional programming language; pretty much universally, the most popular pure functional language.

IDE
Integrated Development Environment. A comprehensive editor containing an internal debugger and runtime environment.

immutable
A data structure (variable, object, etc.) which cannot be changed once the initial value is set.

infinite recursion
When a recursive call has no bounding condition to terminate the loop.

infix operator
An operator (usual a symbol) which can be placed between two arguments. For example, $a ?? $b where ?? is the infix operator.

IO
Input/Output. Generally refers to reading from and writing to disk.

iter
Library to work with PHP's various collections agnostically with generators.

keyword
A word with special significance in a programming language as it may direct control or indicate usage of certain feature.

lambda
An anonymous function (one without a defined name).

λ
See *lambda*.

list
Any data type containing a list of values. May or may not additionally include a key for each value.

monad
A design pattern with a universal interface.

namespace
A virtual grouping of subroutines under a shared name. Allows subroutines with the same name to co-exist under different namespaces.

Netbeans
A JVM based IDE which among other languages supports PHP natively.

null
A value meaning no value and should be avoided (an oxymoron).

null coalescence
A PHP operator which can be placed between two variables and will return the first non-null value.

OCaml
A multi-paradigm programming language allowing functional and object oriented styles of programming. Hack lang is written in it.

PAAS
Platform As A Service is a system which includes scalable hosting and some sort of assistance with the development workflow such as pushing changes live via git.

parameter
See *argument*.

parentheses
()

partial function application
A technique where a function's arguments are supplied as defaults by a wrapping function. Generally, one argument is left as a placeholder which will be substituted at call time. This is very handy when using `array_map()` and `substr()` together, for example.

PEAR
An early PHP library management program and repository. Nowadays superceded in use by Composer and Packagist.

PECL
PHP extension management program and repository.

period
.

PHP extension
These are compilable extensions to PHP written in C. The biggest advantage over a library is outright speed and the ability to implement C APIs.

PHP library
Userland PHP code which can be bolted into a project to add ready-made functionality.

PHPDoc
A popular method of inline code documentation which can be automatically built to an API manual.

PHPSH
Facebook's PHP REPL.

pipelines
A list of functions to be mapped against one or more values.

POSIX
A computer which can interpret the POSIX instruction set. The two most popular are Linux and Mac OS X.

psyPHP
A REPL amongst other things.

pure
Difficult to define, but generally, a function which is referentially transparent.

React/Partial
A userland library which provides partial function application to PHP projects.

recursion
When a function calls itself either directly or indirectly. For an example, see see recursion.

referential transparency
A function is referentially transparent when you can substitute its input for direct values and obtain the same result.

REPL
Read Eval Print Loop. A tool for developers to interactively evaluate code in easily, also referred to as a language shell.

return type
The type of the value a function will emit.

RFC
Request for Comments. In PHP, an RFC must be prepared to accompany any proposed language change or addition. It is then either voted in or out by those with voting karma.

runtime
A system for converting language bytecode into machine runnable instructions. For PHP there are a few including HHVM, Zend (de facto standard) and Quercus.

Scala
A programming language which runs on the Java Virtual Machine and supports both functional and object oriented.

scalar
A category of base types containing one value such as `int` and `string`.

ternary operator
A short form conditional statement which allows for an operation based on a true or false response.

type
The category a value belongs to. 10 is a type of integer, for example.

type definition
A specification of a value's type (int, string, etc.) in code.

type hinting
Specification of a type in locations where a variable is passed in.

use
Either a call to include a specific namespace, to include a PHP trait, or an indication the closure wants to pull in variables from the parent scope at the point of definition.

UTF-8

A unicode/multibyte character standard/table.

UTF-8 ellipsis

…

vim

A text editor suitable for command line interfaces or terminals. Typically available on most Linux distributions, but available for Windows too!

weak typing

Types are transient and the compiler/parser does not care and may at runtime convert between types based on an inferred meaning.

Windows

A Microsoft operating system. If you are using it and following this book install Vagrant and run Ubuntu in a virtual machine to save yourself pain.

xdebug

The go to extension in PHP land for interactive debugging and code profiling.

Index

A

algorithms, 2, 17, 23, 33, 35

annotations, 60, 66

applicatives, 70, 88–94, 148
    context, 91–92
    interface, 89–90
    type class, 89–90

arguments
    list, 28
    name, 147
    supplied, 23, 75

array
    associative, 72
    class notation, 133
    dereference, 135
    filter, 104
    notation, 81
    sorted, 105

Async, 122–24

asynchronous operations, 124, 128

autoloading, 40, 132

B

Babbage, Charles, 1

Barclays Bank, 16

Bletchley Park, 12–13

Boole, George, 10

boolean algebra, 10

C

callbacks, 32, 35, 44, 46, 49, 122, 126, 133

Callback Wrangling, 122–23, 125, 127

cast operator, 21

class
    instance, 36–38
    name, 25–26, 38

closures, 20, 24, 26, 29–34, 36–38, 44–45, 65, 72, 117, 119, 133–34, 140, 144, 152–53, 157
    arguments, 34

code

asynchronous, 117, 126
    imperative, 15, 143
    object oriented, 15, 39

composer, 2–4, 52, 75, 105, 118, 122, 124, 156
    autoload, 4, 52, 105, 118
    automation, 3
    dump-autoload, 4
    init, 3, 118
    install, 4, 51, 118
    update, 51
    vendor, 3, 39

composition, 36, 75, 90, 100

constructor, 63, 95, 111

currying, 12, 36, 76–78
    functionality, 77
    process, 77

D

dependencies, 3–4, 50–53

domain specific languages (DSL), 15–16, 108, 115, 154

DSL. See domain specific languages

E

Elixir, 79

Enigma code, 12

Enum, 59

Erlang, 14, 16

event, 117–18, 120, 122, 124, 126, 128, 130
    loop, 118–19, 127–28

Everest, George, 10

extensions, 2–5, 26, 28, 35, 41, 49–50, 56, 117, 154, 158
    functional-php, 50
    php-immutable, 132

F

Facebook, 3, 5, 55–56

factory, 111, 118

Flat Map, 45–46

flatten, 46, 71–72

Flowers, Tommy, 12

fmap, 84–90

Frege's Basic Law, 10

function
    anonymous, 28–29, 33, 41, 65, 82, 93, 97, 153, 155
    arguments, 26, 28, 56, 60, 81, 136, 138, 147, 154
    basic monad, 120
    body, 24–25
    callback closure, 107
    composable, 69, 100
    compose, 50, 100–101
    higher order, 14
    list/iterable access, 52
    named, 23, 25, 28, 121
    namespacing, 136
    objects, 36, 38, 42, 126, 154
    parameters, 27, 59–60
    pipeline, 78–80
    recursive, 11–12, 40
    return values, 135, 138
    variadic, 135, 149
    wrapped, 88–89, 93
functional languages, 7, 14–16, 29, 69, 93, 131, 147
FunctionalPhp, 140
Functionals, 47, 78, 105, 144
functors, 36, 38, 83, 85–89, 91, 93–94, 96, 134, 148
    law, 87

G

Geheimschreiber, 12
generator, 47–48, 52–53, 134, 154–55
    expressions, 140
    syntax, 47
generics, 59, 62–64
Gödel, Kurt, 11–12

H

Hack, 6, 55–62, 64–67, 154
    language, 3, 55–56
hash, 33, 47
Haskell, 8, 14–16, 80–81, 84, 94, 98, 143, 148, 152, 154
    programming language, 69, 78
    types, 147

HHVM's Hack, 55–56, 58, 60, 62, 64, 66, 68

I

iterators, 48, 52

J

JavaScript, 29, 49, 117
Java Virtual Machine (JVM), 15, 56, 155, 157
Jones, Simon Peyton, 8, 103
JVM. See Java Virtual Machine
Jython, 56

K

key/value list, 20, 58

L

lambda, 28–29, 41, 117, 121, 144, 153, 155
    calculus, 11, 29
    expressions, 11–12, 65–66
    functions, 18, 20, 28–34, 41, 65, 133
lazy loading, 29, 32, 75
libraries
    functional, 50, 69
    php-option, 74, 98
LISP, 13–14, 16
    programming language, 133
logging, 100, 119
Lovelace, Ada, 1

M

map, 14, 32, 35, 42–46, 52–53, 58, 62–63, 70, 72, 76, 79–80, 94–97, 99, 102, 119–20
    ordered, 20, 58
memoize, 47, 66
Monadic Laws, 96
monads, 69–70, 93–99, 101–2, 119–22, 148, 155
    container, 120
    interface, 94
    list, 120
    state, 102
    structure, 94
    writer, 99, 102

N

namespaces, 25
NET framework, 154
Newman, Max, 12

O

object-oriented programming, 16, 29
OCaml, 56, 152, 155
operator, splat, 27–28, 136

P

partial function application, 36, 50, 76–77, 82, 156–57
pattern matching, 15, 80–82
PDO, 98–99
PECL, 2, 5, 50, 156
    extension, 4–5, 49, 117
PHPDaemon, 129
PHPDoc, 145–46, 156
PHP SuperClosure, 29, 152
pipelines, 78–80, 156
primitives, functional, 49–50, 105, 107–8, 154
promises, 124, 126–28
    deferred, 127–28
PsySH, 2, 151
Python, 14, 41, 56

R

React/Async project, 124
React/Partial, 2, 50–51, 76, 149, 152, 157
ReactPHP, 117, 119, 129, 143
recursion, 11, 14, 19–20, 40–41, 44, 70, 157
    direct, 41
    indirect, 41
    infinite, 155
    mutual, 41
recursive form, common, 40
REPL, 2, 156–57
resolver, 125, 127–28
RFC, 66, 106, 135, 138, 140, 144, 157
Russell, Bertrand, 10

S

Scala, 15–16, 49, 80–81, 143, 147–48, 152, 157
    Option values, 74
    programming language, 15, 152
scope, 24, 30, 36–38, 65, 128
    parent, 24–25, 157
state
    avoiding, 117
    global mutable, 7, 41
    maintaining, 9
subroutines, 153–55
superglobals, 24

T

transparency, referential, 8, 17, 157
Turing, 12–13, 16
    Machines, 11–12
    Test, 13
type hints, 23, 25–26, 59, 86, 136–38
    callable, 133
    scalar, 137
    strict, 23
types
    complex, 88
    enumeration, 59
    expected, 147
    Hack, 56
    immutable, 59
    internal, 60
    new, 56, 61
    scalar, 20, 26, 56, 147
    strict, 137
    weak, 69

U

Ubuntu, 3, 5–6, 158
Underscore.php, 50–51, 132, 144
US Secure Hash Algorithm, 33
UTF-8, 113, 121, 158
    Ellipsis, 76, 149, 158

V

values
    carried, 79
    coerce, 147
    primitive, 43
    scalar, 111
variables, global, 25, 30
variadics, 26–28, 135–36
Vector, 58, 62

W

Windows, 6, 149, 158

Z

Zend, 157
    Engine, 56
    runtime, 139
Zephir, 56

php[architect] Books

The php[architect] series of books cover topics relevant to modern PHP programming. We offer our books in both print and digital formats. Print copy price includes free shipping to the US. Books sold digitally are available to you DRM-free in PDF, ePub, or Mobi formats for viewing on any device that supports these.

To view the complete selection of books and order a copy of your own, please visit: *http://phparch.com/books/*.

- **Web Security 2016**
  Edited by Oscar Merida
  ISBN: 978-1940111414

- **Docker for Developers**
  By Chris Tankersley
  ISBN: 978-1940111360 (Print edition)

- **Building Exceptional Sites with WordPress & Thesis**
  By Peter MacIntyre
  ISBN: 978-1940111315

- **Integrating Web Services with OAuth and PHP**
  By Matthew Frost
  ISBN: 978-1940111261

- **Zend Framework 1 to 2 Migration Guide**
  By Bart McLeod
  ISBN: 978-1940111216

- **XML Parsing with PHP**
  By John M. Stokes
  ISBN: 978-1940111162

- **Zend PHP 5 Certification Study Guide, Third Edition**
  By Davey Shafik with Ben Ramsey
  ISBN: 978-1940111100

- **Mastering the SPL Library**
  By Joshua Thijssen
  ISBN: 978-1940111001